D0177709

Favourite
Love Poems

BATSFORD

Praise for Dannie Abse

'This erudite anthology breathes life into love's many
tangled confusions. Beautifully done.'
The Good Book Guide

'The ideal Valentine's Day gift.'
Publishing News

'Abse is a writer of urbane humanity with a seeming interest in every aspect of life.'
The Spectator

On the Booker-nominated
The Strange Case of Dr. Simmonds & Dr. Glas

'Abse has written feelingly on the topic of anti-Semitism before, but never with such satirical
accuracy. Deftly handled.'
The Times Literary Supplement

'Superbly crafted.'
The Jewish Chronicle

'Perfectly tuned . . . A dark London in the shadow of
postwar austerity is the well-realised background to this unnerving tale.'
The Times

Favourite Love Poems

Dannie Abse

BATSFORD

An imprint of Pavilion Books Group Ltd

First published as *Homage to Eros* in Great Britain in 2005 by Robson Books
Published as *Ode to Love* in 2007 by Portico Books

ISBN 9781849942799

A CIP catalogue record for this book is available from the British Library.

10 9 8 7 6 5 4 3 2 1

Printed and bound by GPS Printing Ltd, Slovenia

This book can be ordered direct from the publisher at www.pavilionbooks.com

CONTENTS

INTRODUCTION

Dannie Abse

Two thousand and four hundred years ago Plato spoke of the ancient desire of man to make one of two. In so doing, I may add, he and/or she is likely to say, 'I love you'. No wonder those with the gift of language give homage to Eros by expanding on those three little words in one thousand and more surprising ways. 'If ever two were one, then surely we,' wrote the early American poet, Anne Bradstreet.

What a rich picking there is for an anthologist of love poems, of stories of enduring love and love lost. Not to mention wonderful confessions, often robustly comical, of pure lust, mainly by men, since in past centuries declarations of love or about love were generally a male preserve. Sometimes these declarations are sincere, gallant and heartfelt, the poets hymning the physical attributes and nature of their beloveds. Others speak more in lust than in love, flatter to deceive, hoping that their finely chosen sweet words will edge the adored one into their beds.

THE SONG OF SOLOMON

I am the rose of Sharon,
And the lily of the valleys.

As the lily among thorns,
So is my love among the daughters.

As the apple tree among the trees of the wood,
So is my beloved among the sons.
I sat down under his shadow with great delight,
And his fruit was sweet to my taste.
He brought me to the banqueting house,
And his banner over me was love.
Stay me with flagons, comfort me with apples:
For I am sick of love.
His left hand is under my head,
And his right hand doth embrace me.
I charge you, O ye daughters of Jerusalem,
By the roes, and by the hinds of the field,
That ye stir not up, nor awake my love, till he please.

The voice of my beloved! behold, he cometh
Leaping among the mountains, skipping upon the hills.
My beloved is like a roe or a young hart:
Behold, he standeth behind our wall,
He looketh forth at the windows,
Shewing himself through the lattice.
My beloved spake, and said unto me,
'Rise up, my love, my fair one, and come away.

For, lo, the winter is past,
The rain is over and gone;
The flowers appear on the earth;
The time of the singing of birds is come,
And the voice of the turtle is heard in our land;
The fig tree putteth forth her green figs.
And the vines with the tender grape give a good smell.
Arise, my love, my fair one, and come away.'

(This section of the Song of Solomon comes
from the Authorised Version of the Bible, 1611.)

TO LESBIA

Lesbia, let us live and let us love,
defy the severe tut-tutting elders
who advocate cold restraint, how all must die.

Our sun will set but will not always rise
so kiss me now, here in bed or heather,
before night's numb and endless slumber.

Then let us kiss again one thousand times,
then a hundred times, exceed a thousand more,
for each sweet kiss will another breed

until we do not know which who is who
and happily we'll confuse the number
to keep on kissing, kissing, kissing ever.

Gaius Valerius Catullus
(c. 84 BC–c. 54 BC)

FROM ELEGIES TO CORINNA

In summer's heat and mid-time of the day
To rest my limbs upon a bed I lay;
One window shut, the other open stood,
Which gave such light as twinkles in a wood,
Like twilight glimpse at setting of the sun,
Or night being past and yet not day begun.
Such light to shamefast maidens must be shown,
Where they may sport, and seem to be unknown.
Then came Corinna in a long loose gown,
Her white neck hid with tresses hanging down:
Resembling fair Semiramis going to bed
Or Lais of a thousand wooers sped.
I snatched her gown; being thin, the harm was small,
Yet strived she to be covered therewithal.
And striving thus as one that would be cast,
Betrayed herself, and yielded at the last.
Stark naked as she stood before mine eye,
Not one wen in her body could I spy.
What arms and shoulders did I touch and see,
How apt her breasts were to be touched by me!
How smooth a belly under her waist saw I!

How large a leg, and what a lusty thigh!
To leave the rest, all liked me passing well;
I clinged her naked body, down she fell.
Judge you the rest; being tired she bade me kiss.
Jove send me more such afternoons as this.

Ovid

(c. 43 BC–AD 18)

Translated by Christopher Marlowe

FROM AMORES
(BOOK TWO)

I'd rather be in hell with one woman
than in heaven with all those sexless angels.

Sweet Corinna may deceive me and then we
quarrel – but oh what reconciliations!

True, Desire's lantern burns dimly sometimes
yet with a little oil it soon flares up.

You know how it is: a horse bolts suddenly
and, helpless, the rider tugs at the reins.

Or a yacht is driven back from the shore
when its sails are caught up in gusts of wind.

Well, Cupid's arrows know their own way home.
They feel more at home in me than in their quiver!

Life's on lease. Why settle for eight hours sleep
and ignore delightful, flighty Cupid?

Sleep's a rehearsal for undying Death.
There's time enough for nights of peace. So shoot

on, with one eye closed, mischievous boy,
let your arrows seek my heart forever.

Ovid

(c. 43 BC–AD 18)
Adapted by Dannie Abse

THE RIVER MERCHANT'S WIFE: A LETTER

While my hair was still cut straight across my forehead
I played about the front gate, pulling flowers.
You came by on bamboo stilts, playing horse,
You walked about my seat, playing with blue plums.
And we went on living in the village of Chokan:
Two small people, without dislike or suspicion.

At fourteen I married My Lord you.
I never laughed, being bashful.
Lowering my head, I looked at the wall.
Called to, a thousand times, I never looked back.

At fifteen I stopped scowling,
I desired my dust to be mingled with yours
For ever and for ever and for ever.
Why should I climb the look out?

At sixteen you departed,
You went into far Ku-to-yen, by the river of swirling eddies,
And you have been gone five months.
The monkeys make sorrowful noise overhead.

You dragged your feet when you went out.
By the gate now, the moss is grown, the different mosses,
Too deep to clear them away!
The leaves fall early this autumn, in wind.
The paired butterflies are already yellow with August
Over the grass in the West garden;
They hurt me. I grow older.
If you are coming down through the narrows of the river
    Kiang,
Please let me know beforehand,
And I will come out to meet you
As far as Cho-fu-Sa.

Li Po

(8th century AD)

FROM THE RUBÁIYÁT OF OMAR KHAYYÁM

Awake! for morning in the bowl of night
Has flung the stone that puts the stars to flight:
   And lo! the hunter of the East has caught
The Sultan's turret in a noose of light.

Come, fill the cup, and in the fire of spring
Your winter-garment of repentance fling;
   The bird of time has but a little way
To flutter – and the bird is on the wing.

Whether at Naishápur or Babylon,
Whether the cup with sweet or bitter run,
   The wine of life keeps oozing drop by drop,
The leaves of life keep falling one by one.

And look – a thousand blossoms with the day
Woke – and a thousand scatter'd into clay:
   And this first summer month that brings the rose
Shall take Jamshýd and Kaikobád away.

Well, let it take them! what have we to do
With Kaikobád the Great or Kaikhosrú?
   Let Zál and Rustum bluster as they will,
Or Hátim call to supper – heed not you.

With me along the strip of herbage strown
That just divides the desert from the sown,
  Where name of slave and sultan is forgot –
And peace to Mahmúd on his golden throne!

Here with a loaf of bread beneath the bough,
A flask of wine, a book of verse – and thou
  Beside me singing in the wilderness –
And wilderness is paradise enow!

For in and out, above, about, below,
'Tis nothing but a magic shadow-show
  Play'd in a box whose candle is the sun,
Round which we phantom figures come and go.

Omar Khayyám
(1048–1131)

BOAST POEM

Sunday, skilled in zealous verse I praise the Lord.
Monday, I sing in bed to my busty Nest,
'Such whiteness you are, pear blossom must be jealous.'
Tuesday, scholar Gwladus. Not to love her is a sin.
My couplets she pigeon-coos when I thrust to woo her
till her pale cheeks flush like rosy apple skin.
Wednesday, Generys. Dry old hymns I steal to please her.
Then with passion fruit in season I kneel to ease her.
Thursday, Hunydd, no hesitating lady, she.
One small cherry-englyn and she's my devotee.
Friday, worried Hawis, my epic regular.
She wants no baby, she's gooseberry vehement
till sugared by my poetry of endearment.
Saturday I score and score. One tidy eulogy
and I'm away – I can't brake – through an orchard
I adore. O sweet riot of efflorescence,
let her name be secret for her husband's sake,
my peach of a woman, my vegetarian diet.

O tongue, lick up the juices of the fruit. O teeth
– I've all of mine – be sure my busy tongue keeps quiet.

Hywel ab Owain Gwynedd
(1120–70)

IN PRAISE OF MARRIAGE

Marriage is a sweet state,
I can affirm it by my own experience,
In very truth, I who have a good and wise husband
Whom God helped me to find.
I give thanks to him who will save him for me,
For I can truly feel his great goodness
And for sure the sweet man loves me well.

Throughout that first night in our home,
I could well feel his great goodness,
For he did me no excess
That could hurt me.
But, before it was time to get up,
He kissed me 100 times, this I affirm,
Without exacting further outrage,
And yet for sure the sweet man loves me well.

He used to say to me in his soft language:
'God brought you to me,
Sweet lover, and I think he raised me
To be of use to you.'

And then he did not cease to dream
All night, his conduct was so perfect,
Without seeking other excesses.
And yet for sure the sweet man loves me well.

O Princes, yet he drives me mad
When he tells me he is all mine;
He will destroy me with his gentle ways,
And yet for sure the sweet man loves me well.

Christine de Pisan

(1364–1430)

THEY FLEE FROM ME

They flee from me, that sometime did me seek
With naked foot stalking within my chamber.
Once have I seen them gentle tame and meek
That now are wild and do not once remember
That sometime they have put themselves in danger
To take bread at my hand; and now they range,
Busily seeking in continual change.

Thanked be fortune, it hath been otherwise
Twenty times better. But once especial,
In thin array, after a pleasant guise,
When her loose gown did from her shoulders fall,
And she me caught in her arms long and small,
And therewithal so sweetly did me kiss
And softly said, 'Dear heart, how like you this?'

It was no dream, for I lay broad awaking.
But all is turned now through my gentleness
Into a bitter fashion of forsaking.
And I have leave to go of her goodness,
And she also to use newfangledness.
But since that I unkindly so am served,
How like you this? What hath she now deserved?

Sir Thomas Wyatt
(1503–42)

MY TRUE LOVE
HATH MY HEART

My true love hath my heart and I have his,
By just exchange one for the other given.
I hold his dear, and mine he cannot miss:
There never was a better bargain driven.
His heart in me keeps me and him in one;
My heart in him his thoughts and senses guides;
He loves my heart, for once it was his own;
I cherish his, because in me it bides.
His heart his wound received from my sight;
My heart was wounded with his wounded heart;
For as from me on him his hurt did light.
So still, methought, in me his hurt did smart;
Both equal hurt, in this change sought our bliss:
My true love hath my heart and I have his.

Sir Philip Sidney
(1554–86)

MY LOVE BOUND ME WITH A KISS

My Love bound me with a kiss
    That I should no longer stay;
When I felt so sweet a bliss
    I had less power to part away;
Alas! that women do not know
Kisses make men loath to go.

Yes, she knows it but too well,
    For I heard when Venus' dove
In her ear did softly tell
    That kisses were the seals of love;
O muse not then though it be so,
Kisses make men loath to go.

Wherefore did she thus inflame
    My desires, heat my blood
Instantly to quench the same
    And starve whom she had given food?
Ay, ay, the common sense can show
Kisses make men loath to go.

Had she bid me go at first
    It would ne'er have grieved my heart,
Hope delayed had been the worst;
    But ah to kiss and then to part!
How deep it struck, speak, gods, you know
Kisses make men loath to go.

Anonymous
(16th century)

SINCE THERE'S NO HELP

Since there's no help, come, let us kiss and part.
Nay, I have done, you get no more of me;
And I am glad, yea, glad with all my heart,
That thus so cleanly I myself can free.
Shake hands for ever; cancel all our vows;
And when we meet at any time again,
Be it not seen in either of our brows
That we one jot of former love retain.
Now at the last gasp of Love's latest breath,
When, his pulse failing, Passion speechless lies,
When Faith is kneeling by his bed of death,
And Innocence is closing up his eyes;
Now, if thou would'st, when all have given him over,
From death to life thou might'st him yet recover.

Michael Drayton
(1563–1631)

SO WELL I LOVE THEE

So well I love thee as without thee I
Love nothing; if I might choose, I'd rather die
Than be one day debarred thy company.

Since beasts and plants do grow and live and move,
Beasts are those men that such a life approve:
He only lives that deadly is in love.

The corn, that in the ground is sown, first dies,
And of one seed do many ears arise;
Love, this world's corn, by dying multiplies.

The seeds of love first by thy eyes were thrown
Into a ground untilled, a heart unknown
To bear such fruit, till by thy hands 'twas sown.

Look as your looking-glass by chance may fall,
Divide and break in many pieces small,
And yet shows forth the self-same face in all,

Proportions, features, graces, just the same,
And in the smallest piece as well the name
Of fairest one deserves as in the richest frame;

So all my thoughts are pieces but of you,
Which put together make a glass so true
As I therein no other's face but yours can view.

Michael Drayton

(1563–1631)

THE PASSIONATE SHEPHERD TO HIS LOVE

Come live with me and be my Love,
And we will all the pleasures prove
That hills and valleys, dale and field,
And all the craggy mountains yield.

There will we sit upon the rocks,
And see the shepherds feed their flocks,
By shallow rivers to whose falls
Melodious birds sing madrigals.

There will I make thee beds of roses
And a thousand fragrant posies,
A cap of flowers, and a kirtle
Embroidered all with leaves of myrtle.

A gown made of the finest wool
Which from our pretty lambs we pull;
Fair lined slippers for the cold,
With buckles of the purest gold.

A belt of straw and ivy buds,
With coral clasp and amber studs;
And if these pleasures may thee move,
Come live with me and be my Love.

Thy silver dishes for thy meat
As precious as the gods do eat,
Shall on an ivory table be
Prepared each day for thee and me.

The shepherd swains shall dance and sing
For thy delight each May morning:
If these delights thy mind may move,
Then live with me and be my Love.

Christopher Marlowe
(1564–93)

SONNET 130

My mistress' eyes are nothing like the sun;
Coral is far more red than her lips' red:
If snow be white, why then her breasts are dun;
If hairs be wires, black wires grow on her head.
I have seen roses damask'd, red and white,
But no such roses see I in her cheeks;
And in some perfumes is there more delight
Than in the breath that from my mistress reeks.
I love to hear her speak, yet well I know
That music hath a far more pleasing sound:
I grant I never saw a goddess go;
My mistress, when she walks, treads on the ground.
   And yet, by heaven, I think my love as rare
   As any she belied with false compare.

FROM VENUS AND ADONIS

'Touch but my lips with those fair lips of thine –
Though mine be not so fair, yet are they red –
The kiss shall be thine own as well as mine.
What see'st thou in the ground? hold up thy head;
   Look in mine eyeballs, there thy beauty lies;
   Then why not lips on lips, since eyes in eyes?

'Art thou ashamed to kiss? then wink again,

And I will wink; so shall the day seem night.
Love keeps his revels where there are but twain;
Be bold to play, our sport is not in sight.
   These blue-veined violets whereon we lean
   Never can blab, nor know not what we mean.

'The tender spring upon thy tempting lip
Shews thee unripe; yet mayst thou well be tasted;
Make use of time, let not advantage slip;
Beauty within itself should not be wasted.
   Fair flowers that are not gath'red in their prime
   Rot and consume themselves in little time . . .'

Sometimes she shakes her head and then his hand,
Now gazeth she on him, now on the ground;
Sometime her arms infold him like a band;
She would, he will not in her arms be bound;
   And when from thence he struggles to be gone,
   She locks her lily fingers one in one.

'Fondling,' she saith, 'since I have hemmed thee here
Within the circuit of this ivory pale,
I'll be a park, and thou shalt be my deer;
Feed where thou wilt, on mountain or in dale;
   Graze on my lips, and if those hills be dry,
   Stray lower, where the pleasant fountains lie.

'Within this limit is relief enough,
Sweet bottom-grass and high delightful plain,
Round rising hillocks, brakes obscure and rough,
To shelter thee from tempest and from rain:
   Then be my deer, since I am such a park;
   No dog shall rouse thee, though a thousand bark.'

SONNET 29

When, in disgrace with Fortune and men's eyes,
I all alone beweep my outcast state,
And trouble deaf heaven with my bootless cries,
And look upon myself, and curse my fate,
Wishing me like to one more rich in hope,
Featur'd like him, like him with friends possess'd,
Desiring this man's art, and that man's scope,
With what I most enjoy contented least;
Yet in these thoughts myself almost despising,
Haply I think on thee, – and then my state,
Like to the lark at break of day arising
From sullen earth, sings hymns at heaven's gate;
  For thy sweet love remember'd such wealth brings,
  That then I scorn to change my state with kings.

William Shakespeare
(1564–1616)

MY SWEETEST LESBIA

My sweetest Lesbia, let us live and love,
And though the sager sort our deeds reprove,
Let us not weigh them. Heaven's great lamps do dive
Into their west, and straight again revive;
But, soon as once set is our little light,
Then must we sleep one ever-during night.

If all would lead their lives in love like me,
Then bloody swords and armour should not be;
No drum nor trumpet peaceful sleeps should move,
Unless alarm came from the camp of love.
But fools do live and waste their little light,
And seek with pain their ever-during night.

When timely death my life and fortune ends,
Let not my hearse be vexed with mourning friends;
But let all lovers, rich in triumph, come
And with sweet pastimes grace my happy tomb:
And, Lesbia, close up thou my little light,
And crown with love my ever-during night.

Thomas Campion
(1567–1620)

THE GOOD MORROW

I wonder by my troth, what thou and I
    Did, till we loved? were we not weaned till then,
But sucked on country pleasures, childishly?
    Or snorted we in the seven sleepers' den?
'Twas so; but this, all pleasures fancies be,
If ever any beauty I did see,
Which I desired, and got, 'twas but a dream of thee.

And now good morrow to our waking souls,
    Which watch not one another out of fear;
For love, all love of other sights controls,
    And makes one little room, an everywhere.
Let sea-discoverers to new worlds have gone,
Let maps to others, worlds on worlds have shown,
Let us possess one world, each hath one, and is one.

My face in thine eye, thine in mine appears,
    And true plain hearts do in the faces rest;
Where can we find two better hemispheres
    Without sharp north, without declining west?
Whatever dies, was not mixed equally;
If our two loves be one, or, thou and I
Love so alike that none do slacken, none can die.

John Donne
(1572–1631)

THE FLEA

Mark but this flea, and mark in this
How little that which thou deny'st me is;
Me it suck'd first, and now sucks thee,
And in this flea our two bloods mingled be;
Confess it: this cannot be said
A sin, or shame, or loss of maidenhead,
   Yet this enjoys before it woo,
   And pamper'd swells with one blood made of two,
   And this, alas, is more than we would do.

Oh stay, three lives in one flea spare,
Where we almost, nay more than married are:
This flea is you and I, and this
Our marriage bed, and marriage temple is;
Though parents grudge, and you, we're met
And cloister'd in these living walls of jet.
   Though use make you apt to kill me,
   Let not to that, self-murder added be,
   And sacrilege, three sins in killing three.

Cruel and sudden, hast thou since
Purpled thy nail in blood of innocence?
In what could this flea guilty be,
Except in that drop which it suck'd from thee?

Yet thou triumph'st, and say'st that thou
Find'st not thyself, nor me, the weaker now:
   'Tis true; then learn how false, fears be;
   Just so much honour, when thou yield'st to me,
   Will waste, as this flea's death took life from thee.

John Donne

(1572–1631)

TO THE VIRGINS, TO MAKE MUCH OF TIME

Gather ye rosebuds while ye may,
　Old Time is still a-flying:
And this same flower that smiles today
　Tomorrow will be dying.

The glorious Lamp of Heaven, the Sun,
　The higher he's a-getting,
The sooner will his race be run
　And nearer he's to setting.

That age is best which is the first,
　When youth and blood are warmer;
But being spent, the worse, and worst
　Times still succeed the former.

Then be not coy, but use your time;
　And while ye may, go marry:
For having lost but once your prime,
　You may for ever tarry.

TO HIS MISTRESS OBJECTING TO HIM NEITHER TOYING OR TALKING

You say I love not, 'cause I do not play
Still with your curls, and kiss the time away.
You blame me too, because I can't devise
Some sport, to please those babies in your eyes;
By Love's religion, I must here confess it,
The most I love, when I the least express it.
Small griefs find tongues: full casques are ever found
To give (if any, yet) but little sound.
Deep waters noiseless are; and this we know,
That chiding streams betray small depth below.
So when Love speechless is, she doth express
A depth in love, and that depth, bottomless.
Now since my love is tongue-less, know me such,
Who speak but little, 'cause I love so much.

Robert Herrick
(1591–1674)

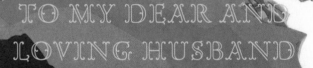

TO MY DEAR AND LOVING HUSBAND

If ever two were one, then surely we.
If ever man were loved by wife, then thee;
If ever wife was happy in a man,
Compare with me ye women if you can.
I prize thy love more than whole mines of gold,
Or all the riches that the East doth hold.
My love is such that rivers cannot quench,
Nor ought but love from thee, give recompense.
Thy love is such I can no way repay,
The heavens reward thee manifold I pray.
Then while we live, in love let's so persever,
That when we live no more, we may live ever.

Anne Bradstreet

(1612–72)

BEFORE THE BIRTH OF ONE OF HER CHILDREN

All things within this fading world hath end,
Adversity doth still our joys attend;
No ties so strong, no friends so dear and sweet,
But with death's parting blow is sure to meet.
The sentence past is most irrevocable,
A common thing, yet oh, inevitable.
How soon, my Dear, death may my steps attend,
How soon't may be thy lot to lose thy friend.
We both are ignorant, yet love bids me
These farewell lines to recommend to thee,
That when that knot's untied that made us one,
I may seem thine, who in effect am none.
And if I see not half my days that's due,
What nature would, God grant to yours and you;
The many faults that well you know I have
Let be interred in my oblivious grave;
If any worth or virtue were in me,
Let that live freshly in thy memory
And when thou feel'st no grief, as I no harms,
Yet love thy dead, who long lay in thine arms.
And when thy loss shall be repaid with gains
Look to my little babes, my dear remains.
And if thou love thyself, or loved'st me,
These O protect from step-dame's injury.
And if chance to thine eyes shall bring this verse,

With some sad sighs honour my absent hearse;
And kiss this paper for thy love's dear sake,
Who with salt tears this last farewell did take.

Anne Bradstreet
(1612–72)

TO HIS COY MISTRESS

Had we but world enough, and time,
This coyness, Lady, were no crime.
We would sit down, and think which way
To walk, and pass our long love's day.
Thou by the Indian Ganges' side
Shouldst rubies find; I by the tide
Of Humber would complain. I would
Love you ten years before the Flood,
And you should, if you please, refuse
Till the conversion of the Jews.
My vegetable love should grow
Vaster than empires and more slow.
A hundred years should go to praise
Thine eyes, and on thy forehead gaze;
Two hundred to adore each breast,
But thirty thousand to the rest;
An age at least to every part,
And the last age should show your heart.
For, Lady, you deserve this state,
Nor would I love at a lower rate.

   But at my back I always hear
Time's winged chariot hurrying near;
And yonder all before us lie
Deserts of vast eternity.
Thy beauty shall no more be found,
Nor, in thy marble vault, shall sound
My echoing song; then worms shall try
That long-preserved virginity,
And your quaint honour turn to dust,
And into ashes all my lust:

The grave's a fine and private place,
But none, I think, do there embrace.
  Now therefore, while the youthful hue
Sits on thy skin like morning dew,
And while thy willing soul transpires
At every pore with instant fires,
Now let us sport us while we may,
And now, like amorous birds of prey,
Rather at once our time devour
Than languish in his slow-chapped power.
Let us roll all our strength and all
Our sweetness up into one ball,
And tear our pleasures with rough strife
Through the iron gates of life;
Thus, though we cannot make our sun
Stand still, yet we will make him run.

Andrew Marvell

(1621–78)

ON LOVING TWO EQUALLY

How strong does my passion flow,
Divided equally twixt two?
Damon had ne'er subdued my heart
Had not Alexis took his part;
Nor could Alexis powerful prove,
Without my Damon's aid, to gain my love.

When my Alexis present is,
Then I for Damon sigh and mourn;
But when Alexis I do miss,
Damon gains nothing but my scorn.
But if it chance that both are by,
For both alike I languish, sigh and die.

Cure then, thou mighty winged god,
This restless fever in my blood;
One-golden-pointed dart take back:

But which, O Cupid, will you take?
If Damon's, all my hopes are crossed;
Or that of my Alexis, I am lost.

Aphra Behn
(1640–89)

FROM
THE HAPPY NIGHT

Since now my Silvia is as kind as fair,
Let wit and joy succeed my dull despair.
Oh, what a night of pleasure was the last,
A full reward for all my troubles past!
And on my head if future mischief fall
This happy night shall make amends for all.
Nay, though my Silvia's love should turn to hate,
I'll think of this, and die contented with my fate.
    Twelve was the lucky minute when we met
And on her bed were close together set;
Though listening spies might be perhaps too near,
Love filled our hearts, there was no room for fear.
Now whilst I strive her melting heart to move
With all the powerful eloquence of love,
In her fair cheeks I saw the colour rise
And an unusual softness in her eyes.
Gently they look, and I with joy adore
That only charm they never had before.
The wounds they made, her tongue was used to heal,
But now these gentle enemies reveal
A secret, which that friend would still conceal.
My eyes, transported too with amorous rage,
Seem fierce with expectation to engage;
But fast she holds my hands, and close her thighs,
And what she longs to do, with frowns denies:
A strange effect on foolish women wrought,
Bred in disguises, and by custom taught;
Custom, that prudence sometimes overrules,

But serves instead of reason to the fools!
Custom, which all the world to slavery brings,
The dull excuse for doing silly things!
She, by this method of her foolish sex,
Is forced awhile me and herself to vex.
But now, when thus we had been struggling long,
Her limbs grow weak, and her desires grow strong.
How can she hold to let the Hero in?
He storms without and Love betrays within.
Her hands at last, to hide her blushes, leave
The fort unguarded, willing to receive
My fierce assault, made with a lover's haste,
Like lightning piercing, and as quickly past.

John Sheffield, Duke of Buckingham
(1648–1721)

FAIR HELEN

I wish I were where Helen lies;
Night and day on me she cries;
O that I were where Helen lies
   On fair Kirconnell lea!

Curst be the heart that thought the thought,
And curst the hand that fired the shot,
When in my arms burd Helen dropt,
   And died to succour me!

O think na but my heart was sair
When my Love dropt down and spak nae mair!
I laid her down wi' meikle care
   On fair Kirconnell lea.

As I went down the water-side,
None but my foe to be my guide,
None but my foe to be my guide,
   On fair Kirconnell lea;

I lighted down my sword to draw,
I hacked him in pieces sma',
I hacked him in pieces sma'
   For her sake that died for me.

O Helen fair, beyond compare!
I'll make a garland of thy hair
Shall bind my heart for evermair
   Until the day I die.

O that I were where Helen lies!
Night and day on me she cries;
Out of my bed she bids me rise,
  Says, 'Haste and come to me!'

  O Helen fair! O Helen chaste!
  If I were with thee I were blest,
  Where thou lies low and takes thy rest
    On fair Kirconnell lea.

  I wish my grave were growing green,
  A winding-sheet drawn ower my een,
  And I in Helen's arms lying,
    On fair Kirconnell lea.

  I wish I were where Helen lies;
  Night and day on me she cries;
  And I am weary of the skies,
    Since my love died for me.

Anonymous
(17th century)

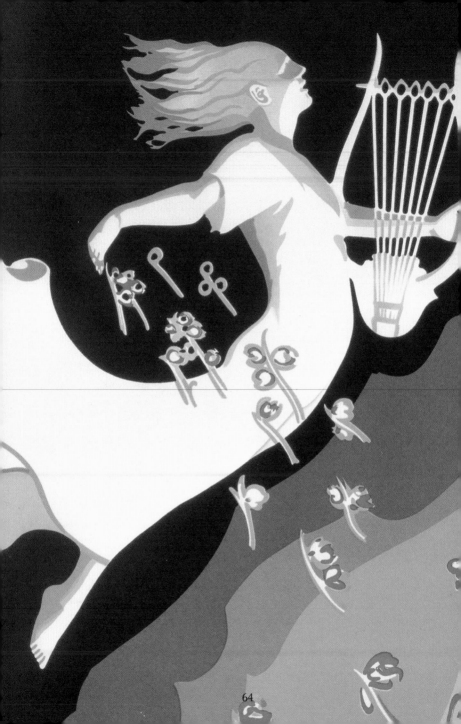

A RED, RED ROSE

O my luve is like a red, red rose
   That's newly sprung in June.
O my luve is like a melodie,
   That's sweetly played in tune.

As fair art thou, my bonnie lass,
   So deep in luve am I;
And I will luve thee still, my dear,
   Till a' the seas gang dry.

Till a' the seas gang dry, my dear,
   And the rocks melt wi' the sun;
And I will luve thee still, my dear,
   Till the sands o' life shall run.

And fair thee weel, my only luve,
   And fair thee weel a while!
And I will come again, my luve,
   Tho' it were ten thousand mile!

Robert Burns
(1759–96)

WHEN WE TWO PARTED

When we two parted
   In silence and tears,
Half broken-hearted
   To sever for years,
Pale grew thy cheek and cold,
   Colder thy kiss;
Truly that hour foretold
   Sorrow to this.

The dew of the morning
   Sunk chill on my brow –
It felt like the warning
   Of what I feel now.
Thy vows are all broken,
   And light is thy fame:
I hear thy name spoken,
   And share in its shame.

They name thee before me,
   A knell to mine ear;
A shudder comes o'er me –
   Why wert thou so dear?
They know not I knew thee,
   Who knew thee too well:–
Long, long shall I rue thee,
   Too deeply to tell.

In secret we met —
   In silence I grieve,
That thy heart could forget,
   Thy spirit deceive.
If I should meet thee
   After long years,
How should I greet thee?
   With silence and tears.

Lord Byron
(1788–1824)

DONNA JULIA'S LETTER

(From Don Juan, Canto I)

They tell me 'tis decided you depart:
   'Tis wise – 'tis well, but not the less a pain;
I have no further claim on your young heart,
   Mine is the victim, and would be again:
To love too much has been the only art
   I used; – I write in haste, and if a stain
Be on this sheet, 'tis not what it appears;
My eyeballs burn and throb, but have no tears.

I loved, I love you; for this love have lost
   State, station, heaven, mankind's, my own esteem,
And yet cannot regret what it hath cost,
   So dear is still the memory of that dream;
Yet, if I name my guilt, 'tis not to boast,
   None can deem harshlier of me than I deem:
I trace this scrawl because I cannot rest –
I've nothing to reproach or to request.

Man's love is of man's life a thing apart,
   'Tis woman's whole existence; man may range
The court, camp, church, the vessel, and the mart;
   Sword, gown, gain, glory, offer in exchange
Pride, fame, ambition, to fill up his heart,
   And few there are whom these cannot estrange;
Men have all these resources, we but one,
To love again, and be again undone.

You will proceed in pleasure, and in pride,
    Beloved and loving many; all is o'er
For me on earth, except some years to hide
    My shame and sorrow deep in my heart's core:
These I could bear, but cannot cast aside
    The passion which still rages as before, –
And so farewell – forgive me, love me – No,
That word is idle now – but let it go.

My breast has been all weakness, is so yet;
    But still I think I can collect my mind;
My blood still rushes where my spirit's set,
    As roll the waves before the settled wind;
My heart is feminine, nor can forget –
    To all, except one image, madly blind,
So shakes the needle, and so stands the pole,
As vibrates my fond heart to my fix'd soul.

I have no more to say, but linger still,
    And yet dare not set my seal upon this sheet,
And yet I may as well the task fulfil,
    My misery can scarce be more complete:
I had not lived till now, could sorrow kill;
    Death shuns the wretch who fain the blow would meet,
And I must even survive this last adieu,
And bear with life, to love and pray for you!

Lord Byron
(1788–1824)

LOVE'S PHILOSOPHY

The Fountains mingle with the River
    And the Rivers with the Ocean;
The winds of Heaven mix for ever
    With a sweet emotion;
Nothing in the world is single;
    All things by a law divine
In one another's being mingle,
    Why not I with thine? –

See the mountains kiss high Heaven
    And the waves clasp one another;
No sister-flower would be forgiven
    If it disdained its brother,
And the sunlight clasps the earth
    And the moonbeams kiss the sea:
What are all these kissings worth
    If thou kiss not me?

Percy Bysshe Shelley
(1792–1822)

TO —

One word is too often profaned
    For me to profane it,
One feeling too falsely disdained
    For thee to disdain it.
One hope is too like despair
    For prudence to smother,
And pity from thee more dear
    Than that from another.

I can give not what men call love,
    But wilt thou accept not
The worship the heart lifts above
    And the Heavens reject not,
The desire of the moth for the star,
    Of the night for the morrow,
The devotion to something afar
    From the sphere of our sorrow?

Percy Bysshe Shelley
(1792–1822)

FIRST LOVE

I ne'er was struck before that hour
   With love so sudden and so sweet,
Her face it bloomed like a sweet flower
   And stole my heart away complete.
My face turned pale as deadly pale,
   My legs refused to walk away,
And when she looked, what could I ail?
   My life and all seemed turned to clay.

And then my blood rushed to my face
   And took my eyesight quite away,
The trees and bushes round the place
   Seemed midnight at noonday.
I could not see a single thing,
   Words from my eyes did start –
They spoke as chords do from the string,
   And blood burnt round my heart.

Are flowers the winter's choice?
   Is love's bed always snow?
She seemed to hear my silent voice,
   Not love's appeals to know.
I never saw so sweet a face
   As that I stood before.
My heart has left its dwelling-place
   And can return no more.

John Clare
(1793–1864)

MARRIED TO A SOLDIER

The pride of all the village,
    The fairest to be seen,
The pride of all the village
    That might have been a queen,
Has bid goodbye to neighbours
    And left the dance and play
And married to a soldier
    And wandered far away.

The cottage is neglected,
    Where young men used to go
And talk about her beauty
    And see her come and go;
The bench agen her cottage
    Where she used to work at eve
Is vanished with the woodbine;
    And all are taken leave.

Her cottage is neglected,
    Her garden gathers green,
The summer comes unnoticed,
    Her flowers are never seen;
There's none to tie a blossom up
    Or clean a weed away;
She's married to a soldier
    And wandered far away.

The neighbours wonder at her,
　　And surely well they may,
To think one so could flatter
　　Her heart to go away.
But the cocked hat and the feather
　　Appeared so very gay,
She bundled clothes together
　　And married far away.

John Clare
(1793–1864)

LAST SONNET

Bright star! would I were steadfast as thou art –
   Not in lone splendour hung aloft the night,
And watching, with eternal lids apart,
   Like Nature's patient, sleepless Eremite,
The moving waters at their priestlike task
   Of pure ablution round earth's human shores,
Or gazing on the new soft-fallen mask
   Of snow upon the mountains and the moors –
No – yet still steadfast, still unchangeable,
   Pillowed upon my fair love's ripening breast,
To feel for ever its soft fall and swell,
   Awake for ever in a sweet unrest,
Still, still to hear her tender-taken breath,
And so live ever – or else swoon to death.

John Keats
(1795–1821)

LA BELLE DAME SANS MERCI

O what can ail thee, knight-at-arms,
   Alone and palely loitering?
The sedge has withered from the lake,
   And no birds sing.

O, what can ail thee, knight-at-arms,
   So haggard and so woe-begone?
The squirrel's granary is full
   And the harvest's done.

I see a lily on thy brow
   With anguish moist and fever dew,
And on thy cheeks a fading rose
   Fast withereth too.

I met a lady in the meads,
   Full beautiful – a faery's child,
Her hair was long, her foot was light,
   And her eyes were wild.

I made a garland for her head,
   And bracelets too, and fragrant zone;
She looked at me as she did love,
   And made sweet moan.

I set her on my pacing steed,
   And nothing else saw all day long,
For sidelong would she bend, and sing
   A faery's song.

She found me roots of relish sweet,
    And honey wild, and manna dew
And sure in language strange she said –
    'I love thee true'.

She took me to her elfin grot,
    And there she wept, and sighed full sore,
And there I shut her wild wild eyes
    With kisses four.

And there she lulled me asleep,
    And there I dreamed – Ah! woe betide!
The latest dream I ever dreamed
    On the cold hill's side.

I saw pale kings and princes too,
    Pale warriors, death-pale were they all;
They cried – 'La Belle Dame sans Merci
    Hath thee in thrall!'

I saw their starved lips in the gloam,
    With horrid warning gaped wide,
And I awoke and found me here,
    On the cold hill's side.

And this is why I sojourn here,
    Alone and palely loitering,
Though the sedge is withered from the lake,
    And no birds sing.

John Keats
(1795–1821)

A WOMAN

Each loved the other beyond belief;
She lived by her wits and he was a thief.
He played the Fool and fooled the crowd;
She sprawled on the bed and laughed aloud.

The days ticked by with joy and with jest;
At night she swooned upon his breast.
When the policeman came, the skies all cloud,
She thought it funny and laughed aloud.

He sent her a letter, 'Oh come to me,
By day and by night I long for thee.
Love is forever, that's what we vowed.'
She shook her head and laughed aloud.

At six in the morning they hung him high
– For fooling and thieving he had to die.
At seven o'clock he lay stiff in his shroud;
And she quaffed red wine and laughed aloud.

Heinrich Heine
(1797–1856)
Adapted by Dannie Abse

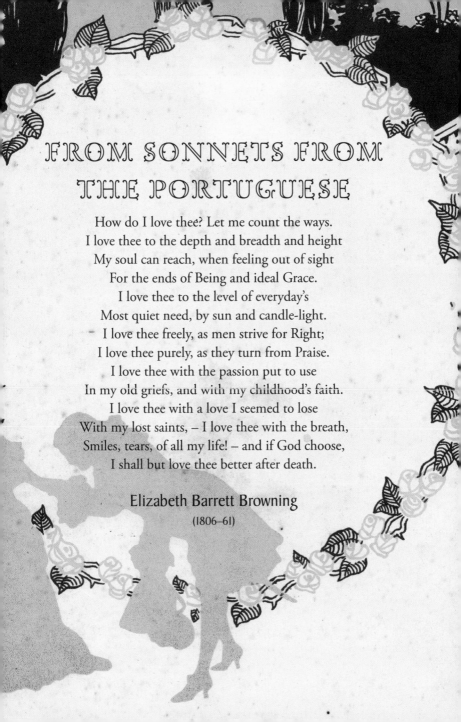

FROM SONNETS FROM THE PORTUGUESE

How do I love thee? Let me count the ways.
I love thee to the depth and breadth and height
My soul can reach, when feeling out of sight
For the ends of Being and ideal Grace.
I love thee to the level of everyday's
Most quiet need, by sun and candle-light.
I love thee freely, as men strive for Right;
I love thee purely, as they turn from Praise.
I love thee with the passion put to use
In my old griefs, and with my childhood's faith.
I love thee with a love I seemed to lose
With my lost saints, – I love thee with the breath,
Smiles, tears, of all my life! – and if God choose,
I shall but love thee better after death.

Elizabeth Barrett Browning

(1806–61)

FROM THE PRINCESS

Come down, O maid, from yonder mountain height:
What pleasure lives in height (the Shepherd sang)
In height and cold, the splendour of the hills?
But cease to move so near the Heavens, and cease
To glide a sunbeam by the blasted Pine,
To sit a star upon the sparkling spire;
And come, for Love is of the valley, come,
For Love is of the valley, come thou down
And find him; by the happy threshold, he,
Or hand in hand with Plenty in the maize,
Or red with spirted purple of the vats,
Or foxlike in the vine; nor cares to walk
With Death and Morning on the silver horns,
Nor wilt thou snare him in the white ravine,
Nor find him dropt upon the firths of ice,
That huddling slant in furrow-cloven falls
To roll the torrent out of dusky doors:
But follow: let the torrent dance thee down
To find him in the valley; let the wild
Lean-headed Eagles yelp alone, and leave
The monstrous ledges there to slope, and spill
Their thousand wreaths of dangling water-smoke,
That like a broken purpose waste in air:
So waste not thou; but come; for all the vales
Await thee; azure pillars of the hearth
Arise to thee; the children call, and I

Thy shepherd pipe, and sweet is every sound,
Sweeter thy voice, but every sound is sweet;
Myriads of rivulets hurrying thro' the lawn,
The moan of doves in immemorial elms,
And murmuring of innumerable bees.

Now sleeps the crimson petal, now the white;
Nor waves the cypress in the palace walk;
Nor winks the gold fin in the porphyry font:
The firefly wakens: waken thou with me.

Now droops the milkwhite peacock like a ghost,
And like a ghost she glimmers on to me.

Now lies the earth all Danae to the stars,
And all thy heart lies open unto me.

Now slides the silent meteor on, and leaves
A shining furrow, as thy thoughts in me.

Now folds the lily all her sweetness up,
And slips into the bosom of the lake:
So fold thyself, my dearest, thou, and slip
Into my bosom and be lost in me.

As thro' the land at eve we went
   And pluck'd the ripen'd ears,
We fell out, my wife and I,
O we fell out, I know not why,
   And kiss'd again with tears.

   And blessings on the falling out
     That all the more endears,
   When we fall out with those we love,
     And kiss again with tears.

   For when we came where lies the child
     We lost in other years,
   There above the little grave
   O there above the little grave,
     We kiss'd again with tears.

Alfred, Lord Tennyson
(1809–92)

A WOMAN'S LAST WORD

Let's contend no more, Love,
    Strive nor weep:
All be as before, Love,
    – Only sleep!

What so wild as words are?
    I and thou
In debate, as birds are,
    Hawk on bough!

See the creature stalking
    While we speak!
Hush and hide the talking,
    Cheek on cheek!

What so false as truth is,
    False to thee?
Where the serpent's tooth is,
    Shun the tree –

Where the apple reddens
    Never pry –
Lest we lose our Edens,
    Eve and I!

Be a god and hold me
    With a charm!
Be a man and fold me
    With thine arm!

Teach me, only teach, Love!
    As I ought
I will speak thy speech, Love,
    Think thy thought –

Meet, if thou require it,
    Both demands,
Laying flesh and spirit
    In thy hands.

That shall be tomorrow
    Not tonight:
I must bury sorrow
    Out of sight:

– Must a little weep, Love,
    (Foolish me!)
And so fall asleep, Love
    Loved by thee.

Robert Browning
(1812–89)

A LIGHT WOMAN

So far as our story approaches the end,
    Which do you pity the most of us three? –
My friend, or the mistress of my friend
    With her wanton eyes, or me?

My friend was already too good to lose,
    And seemed in the way of improvement yet,
When she crossed his path with her hunting-noose
    And over him drew her net.

When I saw him tangled in her toils,
    A shame, said I, if she adds just him
To her nine-and-ninety other spoils,
    The hundredth, for a whim!

And before my friend be wholly hers,
    How easy to prove to him, I said
An eagle's the game her pride prefers,
    Though she snaps at the wren instead!

So, I gave her eyes my own eyes to take,
    My hand sought hers as in earnest need,
And round she turned for my noble sake,
    And gave me herself indeed.

The eagle am I, with my fame in the world,
    The wren is he, with his maiden face.
– You look away and your lip is curled?
    Patience, a moment's space!

For see – my friend goes shaking and white;
    He eyes me as the basilisk:
I have turned, it appears, his day to night,
    Eclipsing his sun's disk.

And I did it, he thinks, as a very thief:
    'Though I love her – that he comprehends –
One should master one's passions, (love in chief)
    And be loyal to one's friends!'

And she – she lies in my hand as tame
    As a pear late basking over a wall;
Just a touch to try and off it came;
    'Tis mine – can I let it fall?

With no mind to eat it, that's the worst!
    Were it thrown in the road, would the case assist?
'Twas quenching a dozen blue-flies' thirst
    When I gave its stalk a twist.

And I, – what I seem to my friend, you see –
    What I soon shall seem to his love, you guess.
What I seem to myself, do you ask of me?
    No hero, I confess.

'Tis an awkward thing to play with souls,
    And matter enough to save one's own.
Yet think of my friend, and the burning coals

He played with for bits of stone!

One likes to show the truth for the truth;
 That the woman was light is very true:
But suppose she says, – Never mind that youth!
 What wrong have I done to you?

Well, any how, here the story stays,
 So far at least as I understand;
And, Robert Browning, you writer of plays,
 Here's a subject made to your hand!

Robert Browning
(1812–89)

REMEMBRANCE

Cold in the earth – and the deep snow piled above thee,
Far, far removed, cold in the dreary grave!
Have I forgot, my only Love, to love thee,
Severed at last by Time's all-severing wave?

Now, when alone, do my thoughts no longer hover
Over the mountains, on that northern shore,
Resting their wings where heath and fern-leaves cover
Thy noble heart for ever, ever more?

Cold in the earth – and fifteen wild Decembers
From those brown hills have melted into spring –
Faithful indeed is the spirit that remembers
After such years of change and suffering!

Sweet love of youth, forgive if I forget thee
While the world's tide is bearing me along:
Other desires and other hopes beset me,
Hopes which obscure, but cannot do thee wrong!

No later light has lightened up my heaven;
No second morn has ever shone for me:
All my life's bliss from thy dear life was given –
All my life's bliss is in the grave with thee.

But, when the days of golden dreams had perished,
And even Despair was powerless to destroy,
Then did I learn how existence should be cherished,
Strengthened, and fed without the aid of joy;

Then did I check the tears of useless passion,
Weaned my young soul from yearning after thine;
Sternly denied its burning wish to hasten
Down to that tomb already more than mine!

And, even yet, I dare not let it languish
Dare not indulge in memory's rapturous pain;
Once drinking deep of that divinest anguish,
How could I seek the empty world again?

Emily Brontë
(1818–48)

SUDDEN LIGHT

I have been here before,
  But when or how I cannot tell:
I know the grass beyond the door,
  The sweet keen smell,
The sighing sound, the lights around the shore.

You have been mine before, –
  How long ago I may not know:
But just when at that swallow's soar
  Your neck turned so,
Some veil did fall – I knew it all of yore.

Then, now, – perchance again! . . .
  O round mine eyes your tresses shake!
Shall we not lie as we have lain
  Thus for Love's sake,
And sleep, and wake, yet never break the chain?

Dante Gabriel Rossetti
(1828–82)

I had a love in soft south land,
  Beloved through April far in May;
He waited on my lightest breath,
  And never dared to say me nay.

He saddened if my cheer was sad,
  But gay he grew if I was gay;
We never differed on a hair,
  My yes his yes, my nay his nay.

The wedding hour was come, the aisles
  Were flushed with sun and flowers that day;
I pacing balanced in my thoughts:
  'It's quite too late to think of nay'. –

My bridegroom answered in his turn,
  Myself had almost answered 'yea':
When through the flashing nave I heard
  A struggle and resounding 'nay'.

Bridemaids and bridegroom shrank in fear,
  But I stood high who stood at bay:
'And if I answer yea, fair Sir,
What man art thou to bar with nay?'

He was a strong man from the north,
  Light-locked, with eyes of dangerous gray:
'Put yea by for another time
In which I will not say thee nay.'

He took me in his strong white arms,
    He bore me on his horse away
O'er crag, morass, and hairbreadth pass,
    But never asked me yea or nay.

He made me fast with book and bell,
    With links of love he makes me stay;
Till now I've neither heart nor power
    Nor will nor wish to say him nay.

SONNET

I wish I could remember that first day,
First hour, first moment of your meeting me,
If bright or dim the season, it might be
Summer or Winter for aught I can say;
So unrecorded did it slip away,
So blind was I to see and foresee,
So dull to mark the budding of my tree
That would not blossom yet for many a May.
If only I could recollect it, such
A day of days! I let it come and go
As traceless as a thaw of byegone snow:
It seemed to mean so little, meant so much;
If only now I could recall that touch,
First touch of hand in hand – Did one but know!

Christina Rossetti
(1830–94)

THE VOICE

Woman much missed, how you call to me, call to me,
Saying that now you are not as you were
When you had changed from the one who was all to me,
But as at first, when our day was fair.

Can it be you that I hear? Let me view you, then,
Standing as when I drew near to the town
Where you would wait for me: yes, as I knew you then,
Even to the original air-blue gown!

Or is it only the breeze, in its listlessness
Travelling across the wet mead to me here,
You being ever dissolved to wan wistlessness,
Heard no more again far or near?

Thus I; faltering forward,
Leaves around me falling,
Wind oozing thin through the thorn from norward
And the woman calling.

Thomas Hardy
(1840–1928)

AFTER A JOURNEY

Hereto I come to view a voiceless ghost;
    Whither, O whither will its whim now draw me?
Up the cliff, down, till I'm lonely, lost,
    And the unseen waters' ejaculations awe me.
Where you will next be there's no knowing,
    Facing round about me everywhere,
      With your nut-coloured hair,
And grey eyes, and rose-flush coming and going.

Yes: I have re-entered your olden haunts at last;
    Through the years, through the dead scenes I have
tracked you;
What have you now found to say of our past –
    Scanned across the dark space wherein I have lacked you?
Summer gave us sweets, but autumn wrought division?
    Things were not lastly as firstly well
      With us twain, you tell?
But all's closed now, despite Time's derision.

I see what you are doing: you are leading me on
    To the spots we knew when we haunted here together,
The waterfall, above which the mist-bow shone
    At the then fair hour in the then fair weather,
And the cave just under, with a voice still so hollow
    That it seems to call out to me from forty years ago,
      When you were all aglow,
And not the thin ghost that I now fraily follow!

Ignorant of what there is flitting here to see,
    The waked birds preen and the seals flop lazily,
Soon you will have, Dear, to vanish from me,
    For the stars close their shutters and the dawn whitens
        hazily.
Trust me, I mind not, though Life lours,
    The bringing me here; nay, bring me here again!
I am just the same as when
Our days were a joy, and our path through flowers.

Thomas Hardy
(1840–1928)
Pentargan Bay

FRANKIE AND JOHNNY

Frankie and Johnny were lovers,
    Lordy, how they could love,
Swore to be true to each other,
    True as the stars up above,
        He was her man, but he done her wrong.

Frankie went down to the corner,
    To buy her a bucket of beer,
Frankie says 'Mister Bartender,
    Has my lovin' Johnny been here?
        He is my man, but he's doing me wrong.'

'I don't want to cause you no trouble
    Don't want to tell you no lie,
I saw your Johnny half-an-hour ago
    Making love to Nelly Bly,
        He is your man, but he's doing you wrong.'

Frankie went down to the hotel
    Looked over the transom so high,
There she saw her lovin' Johnny
    Making love to Nelly Bly.
        He was her man; he was doing her wrong.

Frankie threw back her kimono,
    Pulled out her big forty-four;
Rooty-toot-toot three times she shot
    Right through that hotel door.
        She shot her man, who was doing her wrong.

'Roll me over gently,
   Roll me over slow,
Roll me over on my right side,
   'Cause these bullets hurt me so,
     I was your man, but I done you wrong.'

Bring all your rubber-tyred hearses
   Bring all your rubber-tyred hacks,
They're carrying poor Johnny to the burying ground
   And they ain't gonna bring him back,
     He was her man, but he done her wrong.

Frankie says to the sheriff,
   'What are they going to do?'
The sheriff he said to Frankie,
   'It's the 'lectric chair for you.
     He was your man, and he done you wrong.'

'Put me in that dungeon,
   Put me in that cell,
Put me where the northeast wind
   Blows from the southeast corner of hell,
     I shot my man, 'cause he done me wrong.'

Anonymous
(19th century)

THE FARMER'S BRIDE

Three summers since I chose a maid,
Too young maybe – but more's to do
At harvest-time than bide and woo.
   When us was wed she turned afraid
Of love and me and all things human;
Like the shut of a winter's day
Her smile went out, and 'twasn't a woman –
   More like a little frightened fay.
      One night, in the Fall, she runned away.

'Out 'mong the sheep, her be,' they said.
Should properly have been abed;
   But sure enough she wadn't there
   Lying awake with her wide brown stare.
Over seven-acre field and up-along across the down
   We chased her, flying like a hare
   Before our lanterns. To Church-Town
      All in a shiver and a scare
   We caught her, fetched her home at last
   And turned the key upon her, fast.

She does the work about the house
As well as most, but like a mouse:
   Happy enough to chat and play
   With birds and rabbits and such as they,
   So long as men-folk keep away.
'Not near, not near!' her eyes beseech
When one of us comes within reach.
   The women say that beasts in stall
   Look round like children at her call.
   I've hardly heard her speak at all.

Shy as a leveret, swift as he,
Straight and slight as a young larch tree,
Sweet as the first wild violets, she,
To her wild self. But what to me?

The short days shorten and the oaks are brown,
    The blue smoke rises to the low grey sky.
One leaf in the still air falls slowly down,
    A magpie's spotted feathers lie
On the black earth spread white with rime,
The berries redden up to Christmas-time.
    What's Christmas-time without there be
    Some other in the house than we!

    She sleeps up in the attic there
    Alone, poor maid. 'Tis but a stair
    Betwixt us. Oh! my God! the down,
    The soft young down of her, the brown,
The brown of her – her eyes, her hair, her hair!

Charlotte Mew
(1869–1928)

AND YOU, HELEN

And you, Helen, what should I give you?
So many things I would give you
Had I an infinite great store
Offered me and I stood before
To choose. I would give you youth,
All kinds of loveliness and truth,
A clear eye as good as mine,
Lands, waters, flowers, wine,
As many children as your heart
Might wish for, a far better art
Than mine can be, all you have lost,
Upon the travelling waters tossed,
Or given to me. If I could choose
Freely in that great treasure-house
Anything from any shelf,
I would give you back yourself,
And power to discriminate
What you want and want it not too late,
Many fair days free from care
And heart to enjoy both foul and fair,
And myself, too, if I could find
Where it lay hidden and it proved kind.

Edward Thomas
(1878–1917)

NO ONE SO MUCH AS YOU

No one so much as you
Loves this my clay,
Or would lament as you
Its dying day.

You know me through and through
Though I have not told,
And though with what you know
You are not bold.

None ever was so fair
As I thought you:
Not a word can I bear
Spoken against you.

All that I ever did
For you seemed coarse
Compared with what I hid
Nor put in force.

My eyes scarce dare meet you
Lest they should prove
I but respond to you
And do not love.

We look and understand,
We cannot speak
Except in trifles and
Words most weak.

For I at most accept
Your love, regretting
That is all: I have kept
Only a fretting

That I could not return
All that you gave
And could not ever burn
With the love you have,

Till sometimes it did seem
Better it were
Never to see you more
Than linger here

With only gratitude
Instead of love –
A pine in solitude
Cradling a dove.

Edward Thomas
(1878–1917)

SHE SAID AS WELL TO ME

She said as well to me: 'Why are you ashamed?
That little bit of your chest that shows between
the gap of your shirt, why cover it up?
Why shouldn't your legs and your good strong thighs
be rough and hairy? – I'm glad they are like that.
You are shy, you silly, you silly shy thing.
Men are the shyest creatures, they never will come
out of their covers. Like any snake
slipping into its bed of dead leaves, you hurry into your
        clothes.
And I love you so! Straight and clean and all of a piece is the
        body of a man,
such an instrument, a spade, like a spear, or an oar,
such a joy to me –'
So she laid her hands and pressed them down my sides,
so that I began to wonder over myself, and what I was.

She said to me: 'What an instrument your body!
single and perfectly distinct from everything else!
What a tool in the hands of the Lord!
Only God could have brought it to its shape.
It feels as if his handgrasp, wearing you
had polished you and hollowed you,
hollowed this groove in your sides, grasped you under the
        breasts
and brought you to the very quick of your form,
subtler than an old, soft-worn fiddle-bow.

'When I was a child, I loved my father's riding-whip
that he used so often.
I loved to handle it, it seemed like a near part of him.
So I did his pens, and the jasper seal on his desk.
Something seemed to surge through me when I touched them.

'So it is with you, but here
The joy I feel!
God knows what I feel, but it is joy!
Look, you are clean and fine and singled out!
I admire you so, you are so beautiful: this clean sweep of
      your sides, this firmness, this hard mould!
I would die rather than have it injured with one scar.
I wish I could grip you like the fist of the Lord,
and have you –'

So she said, and I wondered,
feeling trammelled and hurt.
It did not make me free.

Now I say to her: 'No tool, no instrument, no God!
Don't touch me and appreciate me.
It is an infamy.
You would think twice before you touched a weasel on a fence
as it lifts its straight white throat.
Your hand would not be so flig and easy.

Nor the adder we saw asleep with her head on her shoulder,
curled up in the sunshine like a princess;
when she lifted her head in delicate, startled wonder
you did not stretch forward to caress her
though she looked rarely beautiful
and a miracle as she glided delicately away, with such dignity.
And the young bull in the field, with his wrinkled, sad face,
you are afraid if he rises to his feet,
though he is all wistful and pathetic, like a monolith,
        arrested, static.

'Is there nothing in me to make you hesitate?
I tell you there is all these,
And why should you overlook them in me? –'

D.H. Lawrence
(1885–1930)

AN ATTEMPT
AT JEALOUSY

How is your life with the other one,
    simpler, isn't it? One   stroke of the oar
then a long coastline, and soon
    even the memory of me

will be a floating island
    (in the sky, not on the waters):
spirits, spirits, you will be
    sisters, and never lovers.

How is your life with an ordinary
    woman?   without godhead?
Now that your sovereign has
    been deposed (and you have stepped down).

How is your life? Are you fussing?
    flinching? How   do you get up?
The tax of deathless vulgarity
    can you cope with it, poor man?

'Scenes and hysterics   I've had
    enough! I'll rent my own house.'
How is your life with the other one
    now, you that I chose for my own?

More to your taste, more delicious
    is it, your food? Don't moan if you sicken.
How is your life with an image
    you, who walked on Sinai?

How is your life with a stranger
    from this world? Can you (be frank)
love her? Or do you   feel shame
    like Zeus's reins on your forehead?

How is your life? Are you
    healthy? How do you   sing?
How do you deal with the pain
    of an undying conscience, poor man?

How is your life with a piece of market
    stuff, at a steep price?
After Carrara marble,
    how is your life with the dust of

plaster now? (God was hewn from
    stone, but he is smashed to bits.)
How do you live with one of a
    thousand women   after Lilith?

Sated with newness, are you?
    Now you are grown cold to magic,
how is your life with an
    earthly woman, without a sixth

sense? Tell me: are you happy?
    Not? In a shallow pit? How is
your life, my love? Is it as
    hard as mine with another man?

Marina Tsvetaeva

(1892–1941)

Translated by Elaine Feinstein

WITH HER LIPS ONLY

This honest wife, challenged at dusk
At the garden gate, under a moon perhaps,
In scent of honeysuckle, dared to deny
Love to an urgent lover: with her lips only,
Not with her heart. It was no assignation;
Taken aback, what could she say else?
For the children's sake, the lie was venial;
'For the children's sake,' she argued with her conscience.

Yet a mortal lie must follow before dawn:
Challenged as usual in her own bed,
She protests love to an urgent husband,
Not with her heart but with her lips only;
'For the children's sake,' she argues with her conscience,
'For the children' – turning suddenly cold towards them.

Robert Graves
(1895–1985)

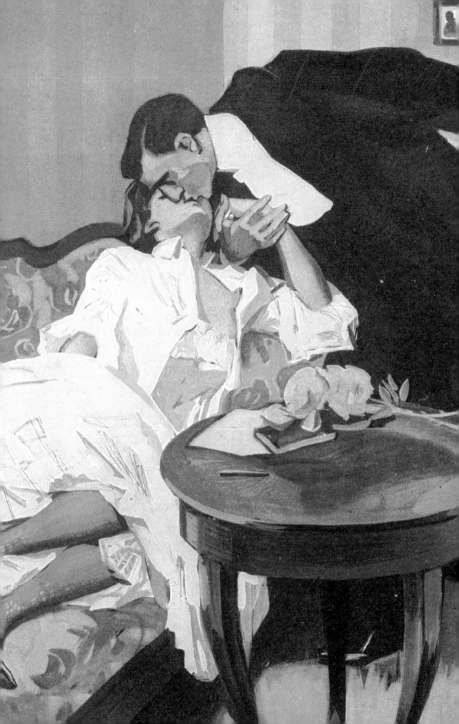

THE FAITHLESS WIFE

So I took her to the river
believing she was a maiden,
but she already had a husband.
It was on Saint James's night
and almost as if I was obliged to.
The lanterns went out
and the crickets lighted up.
In the farthest street corners
I touched her sleeping breasts,
and they opened to me suddenly
like spikes of hyacinth.
The starch of her petticoat
sounded in my ears
like a piece of silk
rent by ten knives.
Without silver light on their foliage
the trees had grown larger
and a horizon of dogs
barked very far from the river.

Past the blackberries,
the reeds and the hawthorn,
underneath her cluster of hair
I made a hollow in the earth.
I took off my tie.
She took off her dress.
I my belt with the revolver.
She her four bodices.
Nor nard nor mother-o'-pearl
have skin so fine,
nor did crystals lit by moon
shine with such brilliance.
Her thighs slipped away from me
like startled fish,
half full of fire,
half full of cold.
That night I ran
on the best of roads
mounted on a nacre mare
without bridle or stirrups.

As a man, I won't repeat
the things she said to me.
The light of understanding
has made me most discreet.
Smeared with sand and kisses
I took her away from the river.
The swords of the lilies
battled with the air.

I behaved just like myself.
Like a proper gipsy.
I gave her a large sewing basket,
of straw-coloured satin,
and I did not fall in love
for although she had a husband
she told me she was a maiden
when I took her to the river.

Federico Garcia Lorca

(1898–1936)

Translated by J.L. Gili and Stephen Spender

COME, LIVE
WITH ME

Come, live with me and be my love,
And we will all the pleasures prove
Of peace and plenty, bed and board,
That chance employment may afford.

I'll handle dainties on the docks
And thou shalt read of summer frocks:
At evening by the sour canals
We'll hope to hear some madrigals.

Care on thy maiden brow shall put
A wreath of wrinkles, and thy foot
Be shod with pain: not silken dress
But toil shall tire thy loveliness.

Hunger shall make thy modest zone
And cheat fond death of all but bone –
If these delights thy mind may move,
Then live with me and be my love.

C. Day Lewis
(1904–72)

LAY YOUR SLEEPING HEAD

Lay your sleeping head, my love,
Human on my faithless arm;
Time and fevers burn away
Individual beauty from
Thoughtful children, and the grave
Proves the child ephemeral:
But in my arms till break of day
Let the living creature lie,
Mortal, guilty, but to me
The entirely beautiful.

Soul and body have no bounds:
To lovers as they lie upon
Her tolerant enchanted slope
In their ordinary swoon,
Grave the vision Venus sends
Of supernatural sympathy,
Universal love and hope;
While an abstract insight wakes
Among the glaciers and the rocks
The hermit's sensual ecstasy.

Certainty, fidelity
On the stroke of midnight pass
Like vibrations of a bell
And fashionable madmen raise
Their pedantic boring cry:
Every farthing of the cost,
All the dreaded cards foretell,
Shall be paid, but from this night
Not a whisper, not a thought,
Not a kiss nor look be lost.

Beauty, midnight, vision dies:
Let the winds of dawn that blow
Softly round your dreaming head
Such a day of sweetness show
Eye and knocking heart may bless,
Find the mortal world enough;
Noons of dryness see you fed
By the involuntary powers,
Nights of insult let you pass
Watched by every human love.

STOP ALL THE CLOCKS

Stop all the clocks, cut off the telephone,
Prevent the dog from barking with a juicy bone,
Silence the pianos and with muffled drum
Bring out the coffin, let the mourners come.

Let aeroplane circle moaning overhead
Scribbling on the sky the message, 'He is Dead'
Put crepe bows round the white necks of the public doves,
Let the traffic policemen wear black cotton gloves.

He was my North, my South, my East and West,
My working week and my Sunday rest,
My noon, my midnight, my talk, my song;
I thought that love would last forever: I was wrong.

The stars are not wanted now; put out every one:
Pack up the moon and dismantle the sun;
Pour away the ocean and sweep up the woods:
For nothing now can ever come to any good.

W. H. Auden
(1907–73)

MEETING POINT

Time was away and somewhere else,
There were two glasses and two chairs
And two people with one pulse
(Somebody stopped the moving stairs):
Time was away and somewhere else.

And they were neither up nor down,
The stream's music did not stop
Flowing through heather, limpid brown,
Although they sat in a coffee shop
And they were neither up nor down.

The bell was silent in the air
Holding its inverted poise –
Between the clang and clang a flower,
A brazen calyx of no noise:
The bell was silent in the air.

The camels crossed the miles of sand
That stretched around the cups and plates;
The desert was their own, they planned
To portion out the stars and dates:
The camels crossed the miles of sand.

Time was away and somewhere else.
The waiter did not come, the clock
Forgot them and the radio waltz
Came out like water from a rock:
Time was away and somewhere else.

Her fingers flicked away the ash
That bloomed again in tropic trees:
Not caring if the markets crash
When they had forests such as these,
Her fingers flicked away the ash.

God or whatever means the Good
Be praised that time can stop like this,
That what the heart has understood
Can verify in the body's peace
God or whatever means the Good.

Time was away and she was here
And life no longer what it was,
The bell was silent in the air
And all the room a glow because
Time was away and she was here.

Louis MacNeice
(1907–63)

GOODBYE

So we must say Goodbye, my darling,
And go, as lovers go, for ever;
Tonight remains, to pack and fix on labels
And make an end of lying down together.

I put a final shilling in the gas,
And watch you slip your dress below your knees
And lie so still I hear your rustling comb
Modulate the autumn in the trees.

And all the countless things I shall remember
Lay mummy-cloths of silence round my head;
I fill the carafe with a drink of water;
You say, 'We paid a guinea for this bed,'

And then, 'We'll leave some gas, a little warmth
For the next resident, and these dry flowers,'
And turn your face away, afraid to speak
The big word, that Eternity is ours.

Your kisses close my eyes and yet you stare
As though God struck a child with nameless fears;
Perhaps the water glitters and discloses
Time's chalice and its limpid useless tears.

Everything we renounce except our selves;
Selfishness is the last of all to go;
Our sighs are exhalations of the earth,
Our footprints leave a track across the snow.

We made the universe to be our home,
Our nostrils took the wind to be our breath,
Our hearts are massive towers of delight,
We stride across the seven seas of death.

Yet when all's done you'll keep the emerald
I placed upon your finger in the street;
And I will keep the patches that you sewed
On my old battledress, my sweet.

Alun Lewis
(1915–44)

Last night I did not fight for sleep
But lay awake from midnight while the world
Turned its slow features to the moving deep
Of darkness, till I knew that you were furled,

Beloved, in the same dark watch as I,
And sixty degrees of longitude beside
Vanished as though a swan in ecstasy
Had spanned the distance from your sleeping side.

And like to swan or moon the whole of Wales
Glided within the parish of my care:
I saw the green tide leap on Cardigan,
Your red yacht riding like a legend there,

And the great mountains, Dafydd and Llewelyn,
Plynlimmon, Cader Idris and Eryri
Threshing the darkness back from head and fin,
And also the small nameless mining valley

Whose slopes are scratched with streets and sprawling graves
Dark in the lap of firwoods and great boulders
Where you lay waiting, listening to the waves –
My hot hands touched your white despondent shoulders

– And then ten thousand miles of daylight grew
Between us, and I heard the wild daws crake
In India's starving throat; whereat I knew
That Time upon the heart can break
But love survives the venom of the snake.

Alun Lewis
(1915–44)

THE OLD FLAME

My old flame, my wife!
Remember our lists of birds?
One morning last summer, I drove
by our house in Maine. It was still
on top of its hill –

Now a red ear of Indian maize
was splashed on the door.
Old Glory with thirteen stripes
hung on a pole. The clapboard
was old-red schoolhouse red.

Inside, a new landlord,
a new wife, a new broom!
Atlantic seaboard antique shop
pewter and plunder
shone in each room.

A new frontier!
No running next door
now to phone the sheriff
for his taxi to Bath
and the State Liquor Store!

No one saw your ghostly
imaginary lover
stare through the window,
and tighten
the scarf at his throat.

Health to the new people,
health to their flag, to their old
restored house on the hill!
Everything had been swept bare,
furnished, garnished and aired.

Everything's changed for the best –
how quivering and fierce we were,
there snowbound together,
simmering like wasps
in our tent of books!

Poor ghost, old love, speak
with your old voice
of flaming insight
that kept us awake all night.
In one bed and apart,

we heard the plow
groaning up hill –
a red light, then a blue,
as it tossed off the snow
to the side of the road.

Robert Lowell
(1917–77)

NO SENSE OF DIRECTION

I have always admired
Those who are sure
Which turning to take,
Who need no guide
Even in war
When thunders shake
The torn terrain,
When battalions of shrill
Stars all desert
And the derelict moon
Goes over the hill:
Eyes chained by the night
They find their way back
As if it were daylight.
Then, on peaceful walks
Over strange wooded ground,
They will find the right track,
Know which of the forks
Will lead to the inn
I would never have found;
For I lack their gift,
Possess almost no
Sense of direction.
And yet I owe
A debt to this lack,
A debt so vast
No reparation
Can ever be made,

For it led me away
From the road I sought
Which would carry me to –
I mistakenly thought –
My true destination:
It made me stray
To this lucky path
That ran like a fuse
And brought me to you
And love's bright, soundless
Detonation.

Vernon Scannell
(1922–2007)

IN SEPTEMBER

Again the golden month, still
Favourite, is renewed;
Once more I'd wind it in a ring
About your finger, pledge myself
Again, my love, my shelter,
My good roof over me,
My strong wall against winter.

Be bread upon my table still
And red wine in my glass; be fire
Upon my hearth. Continue,
My true storm door, continue
To be sweet lock to my key;
Be wife to me, remain
The soft silk on my bed.

Be morning to my pillow,
Multiply my joy. Be my rare coin
For counting, my luck, my
Granary, my promising fair
Sky, my star, the meaning
Of my journey. Be, this year too,
My twelve months long desire.

John Ormond
(1923–90)

DESIGN FOR A QUILT

First let there be a tree, roots taking ground
In bleached and soft blue fabric.
Into the well-aired sky, branches extend
Only to bend away from the turned-back
Edge of linen where day's horizons end;

Branches symmetrical, not over-flaunting
Their leaves (let ordinary swansdown
Be their lining), which in the summertime
Will lie quietly upon her, the girl
This quilt's for, this object of designing;

But such too, when deep frosts veneer
Or winds prise at the slates above her,
Or snows lie in the yard in a black sulk,
That the embroidered cover, couched
And applied with pennants of green silk,

Will still be warm enough that should she stir
To draw a further foliage about her
The encouraged shoots will quicken
And, at her breathing, midnight's spring
Can know new season as they thicken.

Feather-stitch on every bough
A bird, one neat French-knot its eye,
to sing a silent night-long lullaby
And not disturb her or disbud her.
See that the entwining motives run

In and about themselves to bring
To bed the sheens and mossy lawns of Eden;
For I would have a perfect thing
To echo if not equal Paradise
As garden for her true temptation:

So that in future times, recalling
The pleasures of past falling, she'll bequeath it
To one or other of the line,
Bearing her name or mine,
With luck I'll help her make beneath it.

John Ormond
(1923–90)

EPITHALAMION

Singing, today I married my white girl
beautiful in a barley field.
Green on thy finger a grass blade curled,
so with this ring I thee wed, I thee wed,
and send our love to the loveless world
of all the living and all the dead.

Now, no more than vulnerable human,
we, more than one, less than two,
are nearly ourselves in a barley field –
and only love is the rent that's due
though the bailiffs of time return anew
to all the living but not the dead.

Shipwrecked, the sun sinks down harbours
of a sky, unloads its liquid cargoes
of marigolds, and I and my white girl
lie still in the barley – who else wishes
to speak, what more can be said
by all the living against all the dead?

Come then all you wedding guests:
green ghost of trees, gold of barley,
you blackbird priests in the field,
you wind that shakes the pansy head
fluttering on a stalk like a butterfly;
come the living and come the dead.

Listen flowers, birds, winds, worlds,
tell all today that I married
more than a white girl in the barley –
for today I took to my human bed
flower and bird and wind and world,
and all the living and all the dead.

Dannie Abse
(1923–2014)

THE UNDERGROUND

There we were in the vaulted tunnel running,
You in your going-away coat speeding ahead
And me, me then like a fleet god gaining
Upon you before you turned into a reed

Or some new white flower japped with crimson
As the coat flapped wild and button after button
Sprang off and fell in a trail
Between the Underground and the Albert Hall.

Honeymooning, moonlighting, late for the Proms,
Our echoes die in that corridor and now
I come as Hansel came on the moonlit stones
Retracing the path back, lifting the buttons

To end up in a draughty lamplit station
After the trains have gone, the wet track
bared and tensed as I am, all attention
For your step following and damned if I look back.

Seamus Heaney
(1939–2013)

ON THE TABLE

I would like to make it clear that I have bought
this tablecloth with its simple repeating pattern
of dark purple blooms not named by any botanist
because it reminds me of that printed dress you had
the summer we met – a dress you have always said
I never told you I liked. Well I did, you know. I did.
I liked it a lot, whether you were inside it or not.

How did it slip so quietly out of our life?
I hate – I really hate – to think of some other bum
swinging those heavy flower-heads left to right.
I hate even more to think of it mouldering on a tip
or torn to shreds – a piece here wiping a dipstick,
a piece there tied round a crack in a lead pipe.

It's all a long time ago now, darling, a long time,
but tonight just like our first night here I am
with my head light in my hands and my glass full,
staring at the big drowsy petals until they start to swim,
loving them but wishing to lift them aside, unbutton them,
tear them, even, if that's what it takes to get through
to the beautiful, moon-white, warm, wanting skin of you.

Andrew Motion

(1952–)

WHO LOVES YOU

I worry about you travelling in those mystical machines.
Every day people fall from the clouds, dead.
Breathe in and out and in and out easy.
Safety, safely, safe home.

Your photograph is in the fridge, smiles when the light comes on.
All the time people are burnt in the public places.
Rest where the cool trees drop to a gentle shade.
Safety, safely, safe home.

Don't lie down on the sands where the hole in the sky is.
Too many people being gnawed to shreds.
Send me your voice however it comes across oceans.
Safety, safely, safe home.

The loveless men and homeless boys are out there and angry.
Nightly people end their lives in the shortcut.
Walk in the light, steadily hurry towards me.
Safety, safely, safe home. (Who loves you?)
Safety, safely, safe home.

Carol Ann Duffy

(1955–)

VALENTINE

Not a red rose or a satin heart.

I give you an onion.
It is a moon wrapped in brown paper.
It promises light
like the careful undressing of love.

Here.
It will blind you with tears
like a lover.
It will make your reflection
a wobbling photo of grief.

I am trying to be truthful.

Not a cute card or a kissogram.

I give you an onion
Its fierce kiss will stay on your lips,
possessive and faithful
as we are,
for as long as we are.

Take it.
Its platinum loops shrink to a wedding-ring,
if you like.

Lethal
Its scent will cling to your fingers,
cling to your knife.

Carol Ann Duffy

(1955–)

ANTONIA'S STORY

She told me how she fell to sleep with the sound of his fists on
   the door.
Dull thuds that echoed on the stairs,
that became the beat of her heart on the sheet,
the rustle of blood in her ear on the pillow, then sleep.

Of how she slept a dark sleep with only one dream,
of an apple ripening, then falling a fall.
Its loud thud echoing on in the night
in the beat of her heart on the sheet.

And how she woke to the sound of fists on the door
and how she was surprised by the persistence of love.

She told me how she answered the door, and how she
saw him over the policeman's shoulder, lying on the lawn,
and how she thought why is he lying on the lawn, so pale and
   quiet?
Why is he lying asleep and covered in dew?

And then how she saw the broken drainpipe he had tried to
   climb,
and how she knew he had fallen, ripe in the night,
from the broken drainpipe, which still swung wild,
a madman's finger preaching in the wind.

And then she told me how now each night she unlocks the
    door,
which sometimes gets blown, wild in the wind.
How her feet echo, dull on the stairs, as she climbs to bed
where she falls to sleep, the rustle of blood in her ear.

And how each night she sleeps a dark sleep with only one
    dream,
of and apple which falls, ripe in the night.
And of how she wakes with the beat of her heart on the sheet,
surprised by the persistence of love.

Owen Sheers
(1974–)

POET BIOGRAPHIES

The Song Of Solomon (10th century BC) is a dialogue between two smitten lovers. Nowhere else in the Bible is there such a passionate paean of praise for sexual love. No wonder later rabbis and priests attempted to tame its erotic content by interpreting the poem as an allegory of the love of Jehovah for Israel or the union of Christ with the church. It has been claimed that Solomon wrote the poems when he was a romantic youth though no hint of any author appears in the text. The style of the collection relates to love lyrics anciently used at marriage festivals in the Near East and is part of an oral tradition.

Gaius Valerius Catullus (c. 84 BC–c. 54 BC), who is considered Rome's first major lyric poet, was born in Verona. Little is known about him but he probably left his home town for Rome when he was 19 years of age, armed with introductions to Roman literary society. His poems to 'Lesbia' were addressed, in fact, to Clodia Metelli, who was well-born, rich and married. It is thought that Catullus's affair with her began before her husband's death. She was certainly a liberated and promiscuous lady whom Cicero said 'behaved like a prostitute'. That Catullus was smitten by her is evident from his sensual autobiographical poems.

Ovid (c. 43 BC–AD 18) Publio Ovidius Naso, to give him his full name, a Latin poet of the Augustan age. He was 30 years old before he published his first book of poems, Amores, a collection of love poems addressed to a courtesan named Corinna. Ovid's poetry was admired by and influenced such poets as Chaucer, Spenser and Milton. In 1598, Francis Meres wrote, 'The sweete wittie soule of Ovid lives in the mellifluous and honey-tongued Shakespeare.'

Li Po (8th century AD) is generally believed to be the greatest of Chinese poets. He lived a courtly life and was not averse to drinking from 'The Wine-Cup'. Legend has it that while in a boat, intoxicated, he tried to embrace the reflection of the moon in the water and drowned. It was while working on literal Japanese versions of classical Chinese poems that Ezra Pound wrote 'The River Merchant's Wife' by Li Po (Rihaku). How much of this version is by Li Po and how much by Ezra Pound I am not qualified to say. It does not matter. It is a beautiful love poem.

Omar Khayyám (1048–1131) was an 11th-century Persian astronomer poet of Naishápur. His Rubáiyát in English translation was first published anonymously in 1859. Later Edward Fitzgerald acknowledged that he had translated the poem freely from the Persian. Fitzgerald, poet and translator, was a friend of Tennyson, Thackeray and Carlisle.

Hywel ab Owain Gwynedd (1120–1170) Hywel was the illegitimate son of Prince Owain Gwynedd whose kingdom stretched from the river Dyfi to Chester. Only eight poems of Hywel are extant. I have adapted – very freely – one of his best poems. While boasting, he did not eschew the humour of self-mockery. Elsewhere, apart from boasting of his conquest of lovely women, he praised fulsomely the beauty of his native Wales and the bravery of its warriors. Soon after his father died in 1170, Hywel was killed in battle against two of his half-brothers.

Christine de Pisan (1364–1430) was taken from her home in Venice to the French Court of Charles V as a young child. At the age of 15 she married a courtier, Etienne de Castel. In 1389 their happy marriage tragically ended when de Castel died in an epidemic, leaving his 25-year-old wife and three children. She had no inheritance, but by writing about political life in Paris and the plight of women, she admirably succeeded in supporting her family. Her lyrical poems are also of considerable quality. And she could be bitingly ironic.

Sir Thomas Wyatt (1503–42) was a Member of Parliament and diplomat who translated Petrarch and became the first writer of sonnets in English. Wyatt held a number of important posts during the reign of Henry VIII. At one time he was suspected of being Anne Boleyn's lover and, as a consequence, was imprisoned. When ambassador in Spain he was accused of treason and again became a prisoner until he managed to clear his name. Some readers may be baffled by the word 'small' in the second verse of this famous poem. It was a synonym for 'slender' in the 16th century.

Sir Philip Sidney (1554–86) was not only passionate about poetry but was also a man of action. At Court he became a favourite of Queen Elizabeth. When he was listed as a candidate for the crown of Poland, the Queen, afraid of 'losing the jewel of her time', prevented him from accepting the honour. As General of the Cavalry he was mortally wounded in battle against the Spaniards. England mourned him and his remains were brought to St Paul's Cathedral in London for a public funeral.

Michael Drayton (1563–1631), the son of a Warwickshire butcher, being a studious and gifted boy, found rich and influential patrons who supported him through life. It is probable that he studied at Oxford. In 1626 he was styled 'Poet Laureate', but then that title implied no royal appointment. Indeed he paid court to King James but without success. After his death one of his aristocratic patrons erected a gold-inscribed monument to him in Westminster Abbey. The poem 'So well I love thee' was written the night before he died.

Christopher Marlowe (1564–93), who was stabbed to death after a squalid quarrel at a dubious Deptford tavern, is known primarily for the poetry in his plays rather than for his poems. At the age of 23, soon after leaving Cambridge, he was amazing his contemporaries with his grand, rich tragedy, *Tamburlaine*. But, like Shakespeare, he could turn his genius to the writing of quieter love poems when moved to do so.

William Shakespeare (1564–1616) During the last decade of the 16th century, sonnet writing became a fashionable pursuit. Shakespeare's sonnets were published in 1609, but were probably written during 1594 or 1595. Nobody is certain to whom they were addressed. Wordsworth said of the cycle that they unlocked Shakespeare's heart. Though many others have also assumed the sonnets to be autobiographical, it is possible the character depicted in them is as fictional as those in many of the plays. His first published poem was probably the long Ovidian narrative 'Venus and Adonis'. Shakespeare retells the sad, farcical, erotic story of unrequited love, of how the goddess Venus unsuccessfully woos the beautiful boy Adonis.

Thomas Campion (1567–1620) In middle age, Campion studied medicine at the University of Caen. But he was known as a poet and skilled musician who composed music for a number of his own lyrics. During the early years of James I's reign, he wrote a number of court masques. 'My Sweetest Lesbia' is an adaptation of a poem by the Latin poet Catullus 'Vivamus mea Lesbia, atque amemus'.

John Donne (1572–1631) Ben Jonson called him 'The first poet in the world for some things.' Those 'some things' include his unsurpassed love poems and sonnets. In 1601 he clandestinely married Ann More, the niece of his employer, Sir Thomas Egerton, who promptly sacked him. For years Donne suffered economic hardship and was even jailed for a period before family reconciliation. He studied Divinity, Hebrew and Greek and, in 1610, took orders. In 1617 his wife died and Donne wrote little poetry afterwards, instead channelling his talents into the remarkable sermons he gave after becoming Dean of St Paul's Cathedral in 1621.

Robert Herrick (1591–1674) was the son of a wealthy goldsmith in Cheapside who committed suicide when the boy was barely a year old. Fortunately, Herrick had a rich uncle, also a goldsmith, who helped finance his education. Herrick was ordained in 1623 despite his youthful pagan tendencies and later became the clergyman in an isolated village, Dean Prior, in Devonshire. Most of his life he remained there, never marrying, surrounded by many domestic pets and writing love poems to the daughters of the country gentry. For a time he absconded from Devonshire with Tomasin Parsons, some 27 years younger than he and by whom he probably had an illegitimate daughter. He was a master of metre and charming, seemingly simple, love lyrics.

Anne Bradstreet (1612–72) was born in Northampton, England, and educated privately, mainly in religious studies. In 1628 she married the Cambridge-educated Simon Bradstreet. Two years later they left for America and settled in Massachusetts. There, despite her busy family life – she bore eight children – she began to write poetry and prose. In 1650, without her knowledge, her poems were published in London. Partly because of the recent feminist movement and certainly because of her affecting later short poems, her reputation as the first American poet has been secured.

Andrew Marvell (1621–78) No poet other than Marvell could boast of being an MP and a spy. He was elected to Parliament as Member for Hull in 1659. By this time he was already Oliver Cromwell's non-royal laureate. It is thought likely that while in Holland in 1662 he indulged in a little espionage for the British government. Marvell, friend of John Milton, was considered to be a patriot 'whom no bribe could buy and no flattery melt'. The wit and verve of his poetry is wonderfully displayed in this poem.

Aphra Behn (1640–89) was born in Kent to an innkeeper. She married a city merchant of Dutch descent who died less than two years later. During the Dutch war she spied for Charles II. Thereafter she earned her living by writing plays, novels and poetry, the most successful play being The Rover. A visit she had paid to the British colony of Surinam before her marriage later inspired her most popular novel, Oroonoko, or the History of the Royal Slave in which she condemns the slave trade. Virginia Woolf wrote of her, 'All women together ought to let flowers fall on the tomb of Aphra Behn, which is, most scandalously but rather appropriately, in Westminster Abbey, for it was she who earned them the right to speak their minds.'

John Sheffield, 1st Duke of Buckingham and Normanby (7 April 1648 – 24 February 1721), was an English poet and notable Tory politician. He was the author of several essays and of numerous poems, among them the Essay on Poetry and the Essay on Satire, which attacked many notable persons. Sheffield had a scandalous romantic history, marrying three times and having three illegitimate children on the side. His poetic works were published by Pope in 1723.

Robert Burns (1759–96), celebrated poet of Scotland, was the son of a struggling tenant farmer. Largely self-educated, Burns began writing verse while still a boy. His first book led to him being taken up by Edinburgh society. His immediate fame was perhaps partly responsible for this 'Heaven-taught' ploughman leading a life of libidinous excess and amorous entanglements. His radical views were at odds with the dour pieties of the age and his experience of inequality and poverty, along with his natural warmth and generosity of character, find expression in his musical poems whether written in the Scots dialect or in mainstream 18th-century English.

Lord Byron (1788–1824) It was said of this peer that after the publication of the first two Cantos of Childe Harold's Pilgrimage he awoke in London and found himself famous. Young, handsome, athletic – despite having a club foot – he was lionised in society at first until, through scandal, fame became infamy. In 1822, Shelley wrote in private correspondence that Byron 'touched the chord to which a million hearts responded and the coarse music which he produced to please them, disciplined him to the perfection to which he now approaches'. In 1823 Byron sailed to Greece to take part in the liberation of that country from Turkish rule. He died of a fever at Missolonghi, aged 36.

Percy Bysshe Shelley (1792–1822) was a hugely gifted Romantic poet, a rebel who believed in the perfectibility of mankind and who had a passion for reforming the world. Expelled from Oxford University for publishing a tract in favour of atheism, he was later termed 'a rare prodigy of crime and pollution'. Such opprobrium was not only due to his political activity and loathing of religion but also to his abandonment of his young wife who subsequently drowned herself. In 1818, Shelley, with his second wife, Mary, left England for Italy where he resided until drowning when his boat capsized in the Gulf of Spezzia.

John Clare (1793–1864) was born in Helpstone, Northamptonshire, the son of parish paupers. Clare, too, endured poverty throughout his life, working at times as a farm labourer or in the lime-pits at Ryall. He hoped to marry a neighbouring farmer's daughter, Mary Joyce, but her father would not allow it. In 1820 he published his first book of verse in which he described country scenery and rustic events. That year he married Martha 'Patty' Turner, though still in love with Mary. Always of a nervous disposition, his mental health deteriorated until eventually he was certified insane. During his time at Northampton General Asylum, Clare wrote some of his most poignant poems.

John Keats (1795–1821), when dying of tuberculosis, asked of his friend, Joseph Severn, that his gravestone should bear the words, 'Here lies one whose name was writ in water'. But his name is known and will be known as long as English poetry is read. Keats began writing in 1813 and continued to do so while studying medicine at Guy's Hospital in London. Keats's inordinately pronounced identification with suffering patients resulted in him giving up the practice of medicine soon after he qualified. The sonnet included here was written on a blank page in his copy of Shakespeare's poems, facing 'A Lover's Complaint', as he sailed to Italy; he later died in Rome. No doubt Keats had in mind his thwarted love for Fanny Brawne when he wrote it.

Heinrich Heine (1797–1856) was the son of Jewish parents who called him by the rather less Germanic name of Harry. Having been born in Dusseldorf, however, Heine thought of himself as a true Rhinelander. In a letter of 1824, he wrote, that what water was to the fish, German-ness was to him. After 1830, because of German anti-semitism, he settled in Paris, supporting himself by his literary endeavours and writing in both French and German. He became famous for his biting wit, irony and masterly lyrics.

Elizabeth Barrett Browning (1806–61) had a larger public following than her husband, Robert, during her lifetime. She was always of a nervous and delicate constitution and spent many years in her father's house at London's Wimpole Street in the seclusion of an invalid's room. Her 'Sonnets from the Portuguese' were composed during the period Robert was courting her. Despite Elizabeth's authoritative father who would not sanction their marriage, they wed secretly and settled in Italy, mainly in Florence.

Alfred, Lord Tennyson (1809–92) was born of a Lincolnshire family that the poet said 'had black blood in it' and was physically a swarthy gypsy of a man. When eight years old, he imitated the verse of every poet he read. Tennyson once spoke of his mastery of the English language only to add, 'But I have nothing to say.' His lyrics are so melodious and so exquisitely coloured that a reader may well ask, 'Does a jewel need to have a significant philosophy?' His first heterogeneous long poem, 'The Princess', where lyrics – like pearls – thread through the story, was first published in 1847.

Robert Browning (1812–89) is in some ways, along with Walt Whitman, the father of modern poetry. During his early years, like others, he had to endure critical derision. Recognition came later in life. In 1881 a Browning Society was formed to study his muscular, humorous, lyrical and dramatic works. His sense of character was wonderfully fine as is witnessed by his persona poems where he makes his imagined characters speak. His best love poems were written between 1845, when he first met his future wife, and 1861, when she died. He survived Elizabeth for 28 years.

Emily Brontë (1818–48) lived in the parsonage at Haworth, near Bradford, all of her life except for a short period when she was a governess in Halifax. She and her sisters, Charlotte and Anne, wrote poems and prose under masculine pseudonyms, hers being Ellis Bell. She was the most gifted poet of the sisters but her most famous work was the novel *Wuthering Heights*, which was published in 1847, a year before her death from tuberculosis.

Dante Gabriel Rossetti (1828–82), poet and painter, was born in London, the son of a Neapolitan refugee. He was a leading member of the Pre-Raphaelite school and a number of his sonnets refer to works of art. He married his model, Elizabeth Siddal, and when she killed herself in 1862, grief-stricken, he buried his poetry manuscripts in her grave. He exhumed these in 1869 when he published his first book of poems. It has been said of his poems that they 'expressed passion of wedded love in rapture and desolation'.

Christina Rossetti (1830–94) was the younger of Dante Gabriel Rossetti's sisters and the only woman member of the Pre-Raphaelite company. Like her mother she was a devout Anglican and rejected, though not without much heart-searching, two suitors on religious grounds. Her High Anglican piety led her to break off her engagement to a Pre-Raphaelite painter, James Collinson, when he became a Roman Catholic. Living in London, she devoted attention to her mother and aunts in their old age and to service of the church. Because so much of her poetry was preoccupied with death Alice Meynell said, 'Her portrait should have been painted with the skull on the table. Her most admirable poems are fresh and poignant and possess sure musical resonance.'

Thomas Hardy (1840–1928) poet and novelist, the son of a Dorset stonemason, was trained as an architect. But his pressing need was to write – novels and poetry. He was about 20 years old when he began writing verse but his first book, *Wessex Poems*, did not appear until 1898 after he had written several successful novels. During the last years of his life he produced volume after volume of shorter poems – 'lyrical, narrative and reflective'. So prolific was he that his posthumous *Collected Poems* contained more than 900 poems. Among the most personal and poignant poems that he wrote were elegies recollecting his first wife, Emma, who died in 1912.

Carol Ann Duffy (1955–) was born in Glasgow of Irish parents and educated at Liverpool University where she studied philosophy. Recognition of her fresh and accessible poetry came early when she won awards for poets under 30. Soon after she claimed the Dylan Thomas Award and in 1993 the Whitbread Award. Justly, she is now one of the most popular poets in Britain. In 1994 Carol Ann Duffy and I were sent on tour together by Penguin to promote our respective *Selected Poems*. After such poetry readings there were occasions when I felt myself to be merely an admiring, observing chaperone as she charmingly signed book after book!

Owen Sheers (1974–), one of the best young poets to be noticed in recent years, was born in Fiji where he spent much of his childhood before coming to Britain. He studied at Oxford before attending the Creative Writing Programme at the University of East Anglia. His first book of poems was warmly and widely reviewed and won the Vogue Talent Contest for Young Writers as well as a Gregory Award. At present he works for BBC Wales and his second book is awaited with much curiosity.

Charlotte Mew (1869–1928) was born in Bloomsbury, the daughter of a London architect. When her father died – she was then 29 years old – she became a teacher and lived with her mother and sister in genteel poverty. Her first book of poems, *The Farmer's Bride*, appeared when she was 47; her second volume, *The Rambling Sailor*, was published posthumously in 1929. Thomas Hardy and Virginia Woolf called her the greatest living woman poet. There had always been a history of mental instability in her family and, after her mother and sister died, Charlotte Mew took her life by drinking disinfectant while in a nursing home.

Edward Thomas (1878–1917) married Helen Noble while she was still a student at Oxford and decided to make a living by writing. Though he wrote 30 books of poetic prose he and his family lived a life of economic hardship. Persuaded by his friend, Robert Frost, he began writing poetry at the age of 37. Over the next two years he wrote more than 100 poems. His first collection, published under the pseudonym Edward Eastaway, appeared soon after he was killed in the trenches at Arras in 1917. A further volume was published, under his own name, the following year. Thomas's accessible, moving and pleasurable poetry was overlooked for many years.

D. H. Lawrence (1885–1930) 'If you don't like your work, don't do it,' advised Lawrence, the son of a Nottingham miner in a mother-dominated family. And so Lawrence gave up being a schoolmaster to become a full-time author. He began writing poems when he was 19 years old and his best verse may well outlast his celebrated novels. His poetry, like his fiction, is often thinly disguised autobiography. Throughout his writing life Lawrence tried to plumb the depths of the elemental origins of his being and 'to think with the blood'. As Aldous Huxley aptly wrote, after Lawrence had died of tuberculosis, 'He was always intensely aware of the mystery of the world, and the mystery was always to him a numen, divine.'

Marina Tsvetaeva (1892–1941) was the Moscow-born daughter of a Professor of Art and a concert pianist of Polish-German lineage. She began writing verse early and two of her books were published when she was still in her teens. Tsvetaeva reacted strongly against the Revolution as did her husband who fought for the Whites. In 1922 she left Soviet Russia to live in exile. Her autobiographical poetry reflects her nostalgia for Russia and her romantic emotional entanglements. During her last years in Paris, when her husband was too ill to work, she experienced extreme poverty and felt despairingly isolated as a person and neglected as a poet.

Robert Graves (1895–1985) the son of an 'Irish man of Letters' and a German mother, began writing poems at Charterhouse School where he was educated. He continued to write verse after 1914 when he saw active service with the Royal Welch Fusiliers but he did not write satisfying poems until he was middle-aged. Almost a third of the many poems Graves wrote could be classified as 'love poems'. In 1963 he confessed, 'My theme was always the practical impossibility, transcended only by miracle, of absolute love continuing between man and woman.' Apart from poetry he wrote many novels ('To make money,' he said) and an outstanding autobiography, *Goodbye to All That.*

Federico García Lorca (1898–1936) Of all 20th-century Spanish writers Lorca is the most celebrated internationally. His plays and poems are known and revered. He was born in a village near Granada, the son of a wealthy farmer and a culturally sensitive mother who much influenced her son. At one time Lorca dreamed of being a painter and at art school he became a close friend of Salvador Dalí. He was also a gifted musician. But his reputation, of course, is essentially that of a poet and dramatist – one who felt deep sympathy for the oppressed, not least the gipsy people who had settled in the caves of Sacro Monte on the outskirts of Granada. Still in his prime, Lorca, alas, was killed by Franco's fascists soon after the outbreak of the Civil War in 1936.

C. Day Lewis (1904–72) who assumed the pseudonym of Nicholas Blake when writing popular detective novels, was born of Anglo-Irish parentage – his mother being a descendant of Oliver Goldsmith. During the 1930s, when Day Lewis was a schoolmaster, he became associated in the minds of the poetry-reading public with young left-wing poets such as W H Auden and Stephen Spender. 'Come, Live with Me', which parodies the 16th-century love lyric of Christopher Marlowe, was written during the years of mass unemployment. After the war his poems largely ceased to reflect social concerns. He was elected Professor of Poetry at Oxford in 1951 and in 1968 was appointed Poet Laureate.

W. H. Auden (1907–73), the son of a doctor and a former nurse, gained the attention of discerning critics while he was still a student at Oxford. He was a confident youth, one who believed that on reaching crossroads the traffic lights would turn green for him. Like other poets of his generation he had left-wing sympathies and felt strongly enough about the Spanish Civil War that he went to Spain. His subsequent publications alerted the reading public to a poet of remarkable versatile talent. *Another Time* (1940) confirmed his reputation as a major poet of the 20th century. In 1939 he emigrated to the USA and seven years later became an American citizen. Both poems included here are well known – 'Lay your sleeping head' has been much anthologised and 'Stop all the Clocks' was featured in the popular film *Four Weddings and a Funeral*.

Louis MacNeice (1907–63) The Belfast-born classical scholar and son of a Church of Ireland clergyman worked most of his adult life for BBC Radio, writing and producing acclaimed radio features. He used to be described as a dandy, but when I met him in the 1950s his appearance was akin to one of those down-at-heel ex-public schoolboys who appear in some Graham Greene novels! His poetry, however, was always elegant, charming and enjoyable, as can readily be seen in his *Collected Poems* which appeared three years after his untimely death.

Alun Lewis (1915–44) poet and short story writer, was born at Aberdare in South Wales where many a youngster was destined to become a coal miner. Lewis, however, won a scholarship to Cowbridge Grammar School and continued his education at Aberystwyth University where he studied medieval history. In 1941 he was called up for war-service and in that same year married Gweno Ellis. Soon after he was posted to India. He never came back. Like the First World War poet Edward Thomas, whom he so admired, Lewis suffered from black moods. It seems likely that Alun Lewis, lonely and dejected, shot himself – that it was not an accident as officially recorded. His two books of poems, *Raiders Dawn* and *Ha! Ha! Among the Trumpets*, give witness to an important talent prematurely lost.

Robert Lowell (1917–77) was born into an old aristocratic Boston family – the Lowells, it was said, talked only to the Cabots and the Cabots talked only to God! Robert Lowell was educated initially at Harvard and then at Kenyon College, Ohio, where he was influenced and helped by the poet and critic John Crowe Ransome. During the Second World War he was jailed as a conscientious objector and his pacifism later led him to protest about the war in Vietnam. Lowell's early poetry was formal and costive but with *Life Studies* (1959) he broke free from traditional restraints and soon earned the reputation of being the greatest American poet of his time.

Vernon Scannell (1922–2007) In his autobiographical writings Vernon Scannell tells of his experiences as a wartime soldier and a professional boxer. Most of his working life, though, he was a freelance broadcaster and writer whose poetry showed continual dexterity and inventiveness. He took the advice of Thomas Hardy who wrote, 'The ultimate aim of the poet should be to touch our hearts by showing his own.' He won a number of literary awards and was granted a Civil List pension for services to literature in 1980.

John Ormond (1923–90) was born in a village near Swansea. As a young poet his work was too influenced by the poetry of his older neighbours, Dylan Thomas and Vernon Watkins. After a long silence he reinvented himself, even using a different surname. By then (1964) his poetry voice had become singularly his own. A verbally fastidious poet – he was also a gifted BBC Wales film-maker – he revised his eloquent poetry obsessively, saying, 'You cannot play a tune on a slack string.' A plaque outside the house where he lived in Cardiff signifies how highly he is regarded in his native country.

Dannie Abse (1923–2014) 'Epithalamion' is an early poem that I wrote while I was still a medical student. It pleases me that it is used from time to time at secular weddings. 'Epithalamion' is reprinted here at the request of the publisher.

Seamus Heaney (1939–2013), the renowned Irish poet, was the eldest of nine children whose father was a farmer and cattle dealer. Seamus Heaney read English at Queen's University, Belfast, where he became associated with a group of poetry-writing students. Heaney told how they used 'to talk poetry day after day with an intensity and prejudice that cannot but have left a mark on all of us'. His first book of poems, *Death of a Naturalist*, was published in 1966. It happened that I reviewed this volume and I can boast that, like others, I gave it an excellent notice! Further books of poems followed to consolidate Heaney's high reputation. This most articulate of poets was awarded the Nobel Prize for literature in 1995.

Andrew Motion (1952–) It was ironic that Andrew Motion should have been chosen as Poet Laureate – that is one who is expected to produce poems on significant occasions, royal and otherwise – for he is essentially a poet most himself when focusing on personal matters, the stuff of childhood, marital life and past encounters. On the other hand, he did win the Newdigate Prize while a student at Oxford, a prize which requires a poet to have the ability to write on a given subject with true craftsmanship. He is also a commended biographer of John Keats and Philip Larkin.

ACKNOWLEDGEMENTS

For permission to reprint poems in this anthology acknowledgement is made to the following:

Dannie Abse, 'Epithalamion' from *New Selected Poems*, Hutchinson (2009). Reproduced with kind permission of United Agents. W H Auden, 'Lay your sleeping head' and 'Stop all the clocks' from *Collected Poems*, Faber & Faber (1994). Reproduced with kind permission of Curtis Brown. Carol Ann Duffy, 'Who loves you' and 'Valentine' from *New Selected Poems*, Picador (2009). Reproduced with kind permission of Rogers, Coleridge & White. Robert Graves, 'With her lips only' from *The Complete Poems*, Penguin Classics (2003). Reproduced with kind permission of Carcanet. Seamus Heaney, 'The Underground' from *Station Island*, Faber & Faber (2001). Reproduced with kind permission of Faber & Faber. Alun Lewis, 'In Hospital: Poona (1)' and 'Goodbye' from *Collected Poems*, Seren (2007). Reproduced with kind permission of Seren Books. C Day Lewis, 'Come, live with me' from *Ode to Love*, Portico (2007). Reproduced with kind permission of Peters, Fraser & Dunlop. Robert Lowell, 'The Old Flame' from *Selected Poems*, Farrar, Straus and Giroux (2007). Reproduced with kind permission of Farrar, Straus and Giroux. Louis MacNeice, 'Meeting Point' from *Collected Poems*, Faber & Faber (2007). Reproduced with kind permission of David Higham Associates. Andrew Motion, 'On the table' from *Salt Water*, Faber & Faber (1997). Reproduced with kind permission of William Morris Endeavor (UK). John Ormond, 'Design for a Quilt' and 'In September' from *Selected Poems*, Seren (1995). Reproduced with kind permission of Seren Books. Vernon Scannell, 'No sense of direction' from *Collected Poems 1950-1993*, Faber & Faber (2010). Reproduced with kind permission of the Estate of Vernon Scannell. Owen Sheers, 'Antonia's Story' from *The Blue Book*, Seren (2000). Reproduced with kind permission of Rogers, Coleridge & White.

PICTURE CREDITS

© **Mary Evans:** page 11, page 17, page 34, page 40, page 56, page 71, page 77, page 81, page 85, page 95, page 97, page 121, pages 128-129, page 183

© **London Transport Museum Collection:** page 20, page 30, pages 64-65, page 101, page 104, page 110, page 132, page 143, page 151, page 188

© **Science and Society:** page 26, page 45, page 53, page 86, page 119, page 136

INDEX TO POETS

INDEX TO POEMS